The Revolution before the Revolution

Protest, Culture and Society

General editors:

Kathrin Fahlenbrach, Institute for Media and Communication, University of Hamburg
Martin Klimke, New York University, Abu Dhabi
Joachim Scharloth, Technische Universität Dresden, Germany

Protest movements have been recognized as significant contributors to processes of political participation and transformations of culture and value systems, as well as to the development of both a national and transnational civil society.

This series brings together the various innovative approaches to phenomena of social change, protest and dissent which have emerged in recent years, from an interdisciplinary perspective. It contextualizes social protest and cultures of dissent in larger political processes and socio-cultural transformations by examining the influence of historical trajectories and the response of various segments of society, political and legal institutions, on a national and international level. In doing so, the series offers a more comprehensive and multi-dimensional view of historical and cultural change in the twentieth and twenty-first centuries.

The Revolution before the Revolution

Late Authoritarianism and
Student Protest in Portugal

Guya Accornero

berghahn
NEW YORK · OXFORD
www.berghahnbooks.com

First published in 2016 by
Berghahn Books
www.berghahnbooks.com

© 2016, 2021 Guya Accornero
First paperback edition published in 2021

Library of Congress Cataloging-in-Publication Data

Names: Accornero, Guya, author.
Title: The revolution before the revolution : late authoritarianism and student
protest in Portugal / Guya Accornero.
Description: New York : Berghahn Books, 2016. | Series: Protest, culture and
society ; 18 | Includes bibliographical references and index.
Identifiers: LCCN 2015041497 (print) | LCCN 2015047647 (ebook) | ISBN
9781785331145 (hardback : alk. paper) | ISBN 9781785331152 (ebook)
Subjects: LCSH: Portugal--History--Revolution, 1974--Protest movements. |
Student movements--Portugal--20th century. | Student protestors--Portugal
--20th century. | Processo Revolucionâario Em Curso. | Portugal--Politics
and government--1933-1974.
Classification: LCC DP680 .A6245 2016 (print) | LCC DP680 (ebook) |
DDC 946.904/3--dc23
LC record available at http://lccn.loc.gov/2015041497

British Library Cataloguing in Publication Data

A catalogue record for this book is available from the British Library

ISBN 978-1-78533-114-5 hardback
ISBN 978-1-80073-010-6 paperback
ISBN 978-1-78533-115-2 ebook

This work was supported by the Fundação para a Ciência e a Tecnologia
under the grant IF/00223/2012/CP0194/CT0001.
The manuscript was translated from Portuguese
by Andrea Titterington Cravinho.

To my grandfather, Mario Cantele, partisan

Contents

Figures

Acknowledgments

Many are the people who have accompanied me in the adventure of this book, before the research phase, after its writing and finally in the editing process. Among them, I wish to particularly acknowledge Professor Manuel Villaverde Cabral, and for innumerable reasons. Not only was he an inexorable source of intellectual stimuli, who always managed – in an almost Socratic form – to help me to place in writing the issues and disquietudes brooding in my mind during this work, but he has also been an indispensable human reference, always present over the last ten years. I would also like to acknowledge all my friends who, each in their own way, have accompanied me on this journey. In the first place, Diego Palacios Cerezales, who followed the development of my research since the very beginning, over a beer or two, both in Lisbon and Madrid. Likewise, I would to thank Pedro Ramos Pinto, who always gave me self-confidence and warm encouragement, both for the writing of this book and in the work that we have conducted jointly over these last few years. My gratitude is also expressed to all my friends who have over these years become my new 'Lisbon family', among the others: Giulia Strippoli, Catherine Moury, Joana Azevedo, Sofia Sampaio, AnnaRita Gori, Chiara Carrozza, Micaela Cacciarelli, Riccardo Marchi, Marco Allegra, Vania Baldi, Frédéric Vidal, Antoine Burlet.

My acknowledgements could not fail to include the FCT that has financed my work over the last ten years, as well as the ICS-UL, the institute where I carried out the investigation at the base of this book, and the CIES-IUL, the centre where I have worked since 2010. I also extend my gratitude to Berghahn Books for their professionalism, as well as to the three anonymous reviewers who read my book and whose suggestions were extremely helpful in its improvement.

Finally, a very special thank you to Goffredo Adinolfi, for strongly encouraging me to begin this journey.

Abbreviations

AAC	Associação Académica de Coimbra (Coimbra Academic Association)
AEESBAP	Associação de Estudantes da Escola Superior de Belas Artes do Porto (Student Association of High School for the Fine Arts of Oporto)
AEFDL	Associação de Estudantes da Faculdade de Direito de Lisboa (Student Association of the Faculty of Law of Lisbon).
AEFML	Associação de Estudantes da Faculdade de Medicina de Lisboa (Student Association of Faculty of Medicine of Lisbon)
AEISCEF	Associação dos Estudantes do Instituto Superior de Ciências Económicas e Financeiras (Student Association of the School of Economics and Management of Lisbon)
AEIST	Associação de Estudantes do Instituto Superior Técnico (Student Association of the Higher Technical Institute)
AHM	Arquivo Histórico Militar (Historical Military Archive)
AHS-ICS/UL	Arquivo de História Social do Instituto de Ciências Sociais da Universidade de Lisboa (Social History Archive of the Institute of Social Science of the University of Lisbon)
AN	Assembleia Nacional (National Assembly)
ANP	Acção Nacional Popular (National Popular Action)
ARA	Acção Revolucionária Armada (Revolutionary Armed Action)
ASP	Acção Socialista Portuguesa (Portuguese Socialist Association)
BR	Brigadas Revolucionárias (Revolutionary Brigades)
CADC	Centro Académico de Democracia Cristã (Academic Centre of the Christian Democracy)
CARPML	Comité de Apoio à Reorganização do Partido Marxista–Leninista (Support Committee for the Reorganization of the Marxist-Leninist Party)

CCRML	Comités Comunistas Revolucionários Marxistas–Leninistas (Communist Revolutionary Marxist-Leninist Committees)
CDE	Comissão Democrática Eleitoral (Democratic Electoral Commission).
CDS-PP	Centro Democrático Social – Partido Popular (Social Democratic Centre – Popular Party)
CEDL	Comissão dos Estudantes Democráticos de Lisboa (Democratic Students Commission of Lisbon)
CEM	Comissão Eleitoral Monárquica (Monarchist Electoral Commission)
CEUD	Comissão Eleitoral de Unidade Democrática (Electoral Commission of Democratic Unity)
CGIL	Confederazione Generale Italiana del Lavoro (Italian General Confederation of Labour)
CGTP-IN	Confederação Geral dos Trabalhadores Portugueses-Intersindical (General Confederation of the Portuguese Workers National Trades Union)
CIA	Comissão Inter Associações (Inter-Associations Commission)
CIES	Centro de Investigação e Estudo de Sociologia (Centre of Research and Studies in Sociology)
CITAC	Círculo de Iniciação Teatral Académica de Coimbra (Society for the Academic Introduction to Theatre of Coimbra).
CLAC	Comités de Luta Anti-Colonial (Committee of Anti-Colonial Fight)
CMLP	Comité Marxista Leninista Português (Portuguese Marxist Leninist Committee)
COPCON	Comando Operacional do Continente (Continental Operations Command)
CPC	Communist Party of China
CPRAAC	Comissão Pró Reabertura da Associação Académica de Coimbra (Commission for the Re-Opening of the Academic Association of Coimbra).
CPSU	Communist Party of the Soviet Union
CR	Conselho das Repúblicas (Council of Republics)

CREC	Comité Revolucionário dos Estudantes Comunistas (Revolutionary Committee of Communist Students)
DG	Direcção Geral (General Directorate)
DGAAC	Direcção Geral da Associação Académica de Coimbra (General Directorate of the Academic Association of Coimbra)
DGS	Direcção Geral de Segurança (General Directorate for Security)
DN	*Diário de Notícias*
DRIL	Directorio Revolucionario Ibérico de Liberación (Iberian Revolutionary Directorate for Liberation)
EDE	Esquerda Democrática Estudantil (Student Democratic Left)
FAP	Frente de Acção Popular (Popular Action Front)
FCT	Fundação para a Ciência e a Tecnologia (Foundation for Science and Technology)
FEML	Federação dos Estudantes Marxistas–Leninistas (Marxist-Leninist Students Federation)
FEUP	Faculdade de Engenharia da Universidade do Porto (Faculty of Medicin of the University of Oporto)
FJCP	Federação Juvenil Comunista Portuguesa (Portuguese Communist Portuguese Youth)
FPLN	Frente Patriótica de Libertação Nacional (Patriotic Front of National Liberation)
GNR	Guarda Nacional Republicana (National Republican Guard)
GSR	Grupo Socialista Revolucionário (Revolutionary Socialist Group)
IAEM	Instituto de Altos Estudos Militares (Institute of Advanced Military Studies)
IAN/TT	Instituto dos Arquivos Nacionais Torre do Tombo (Torre do Tombo National Archive Institute)
ICS	Instituto de Ciências Sociais da Universidade de Lisboa (Social Science Institute of the University of Lisbon)
ISCEF	Instituto Superior de Ciências Económicas e Financeiras (Higher Institute of Economic and Financial Sciences)
IST	Instituto Superior Técnico (Higher Technical Institute)
JAP	Juntas de Acção Patriótica (Patriotic Action Junta)

JCP	Juventude Comunista Portuguesa (Portuguese Communist Youth)
JSN	Junta de Salvação Nacional (National Salvation Junta)
JUC	Juventude Universitária Católica (University Catholic Youth)
LP	Legião Portuguesa (Portuguese Legion)
LUAR	Liga de União e Acção Revolucionária (League of Unity and Revolutionary Action)
MAR	Movimento de Acção Revolucionária (Revolutionary Action Mouvement)
MDE	Movimento Democrático Estudantil (Students Democratic Movement)
MEN	Ministério da Educação Nacional (Ministry of National Education)
MFA	Movimento das Forças Armadas (Armed Forces Movement)
MI	Ministério do Interior (Home Office)
MLM	Movimento de Libertação das Mulheres (Women Liberation Movement)
MND	Movimento Nacional Democrático (Democratic National Movement)
MNE	Movimento Nacional de Estudantes (Students National Movement)
MNI	Movimento Nacional Independente (Independent National Movement)
MP	Mocidade Portuguesa (Portuguese Youth)
MPAC	Movimento Popular Anti-Colonial (Anti-Colonial Popular Movement)
MPLA	Movimento Popular de Libertação da Angola (Movement for the Liberation of Angola)
MRPP	Movimento Reorganizativo do Partido do Proletariado (Reorganized Movement of the Party of the Proletariat)
MSI	Movimento Sociale Italiano (Italian Social Movement)
MUD	Movimento de Unidade Democrática (Movement of Democratic Unity)
MUDJ	Movimento de Unidade Democrática Juvenil (Movement for Democratic Youth Unity)

MVSN	Milizia Volontaria per la Sicurezza Nazionale (Voluntary Militia for National Security)
OCMLP	Organização Comunista Marxista-Leninista Portuguesa (Portuguese Communist Marxist-Leninist Organization)
OVRA	Opera Volontaria per la Repressione dell'Antifascismo (Voluntary Work for the Repression of Antifascism) *or* Organizzazione di Vigilanza e Repressione dell'Antifascismo (Organization of Surveillance and Repression of Antifascism), *or* Organo di Vigilanza dei Reati Antistatali (Surveillance Body of Crimes Against the State)
PCI	Partito Comunista Italiano (Italian Communist Party)
PCP	Partido Comunista Português (Portuguese Communist Party)
PCP-ML	Partido Comunista de Portugal Marxista–Leninista (Communist Party of Portugal Marxist-Leninist)
PIDE	Polícia Internacional de Defesa do Estado (International and State Defence Police)
PJ	Polícia Judiciária (Judicial Police)
POS	Political Opportunity Structure
PPD	Partido Popular Democrático (Popular Democratic Party)
PREC	Processo Revolucionário em Curso (Revolutionary Process Underway)
PRP	Partido Revolucionário do Proletariado (Revolutionary Party of the Proletariat)
PS	Partido Socialista (Socialist Party)
PSD	Partido Social Democrata (Social Democratic Party)
PSP	Polícia de Segurança Pública (Public Security Police)
PVDE	Polícia de Vigilância e Defesa do Estado (Surveillance and State Defence Police)
RIA	Reuniões Inter Associações (Inter-Association Meeting)
RRS	Resistência Republicana e Socialista (Republican and Socialist Resistance)
RTP	Rádio Televisão Portuguesa (Portuguese Radio and Television)
SA	Sturmabteilung (Storm Detachment)
SNI	Secretariado Nacional da Informação (National Secretariat of Information)

SPN	Secretariado da Propaganda Nacional (Secretariat of National Propaganda)
TAP	Transportes Aéreos Portugueses (Portuguese Air Transport)
TEUC	Teatro dos Estudantes da Universidade de Coimbra (Theatre of Students of University of Coimbra)
UCRPML	União Comunista para a Reconstrução do Partido Marxista-Leninista (Communist Union for the Reconstitution of the Marxist-Leninist Party)
UEC-ML	União dos Estudantes Comunistas Marxistas–Leninistas (Union of Communist Marxist-Leninist Students)
UJP	União da Juventude Portuguesa (Portuguese Youth Union)
UN	União Nacional (National Union)
UPA	União dos Povos de Angola (Union of Peoples of Angola)
UR-ML	União Revolucionária Marxista–Leninista (Marxist-Leninist Revolutionary Union)

Introduction

The Student Effervescence

As other European countries, Portugal lived for a long time under right-wing authoritarianism. The military dictatorship established in 1926 was replaced, in 1933, with a regime called the New State (*Estado Novo*) – institutionalized by António de Oliveira Salazar and in force until 1974. During this period, the Portuguese authoritarian institutions faced strong waves of contention on various occasions and carried on by different opponents. Among these opponents, students had gained increasing importance since the mid-1950s and, as of the second half of the 1960s, started to represent one of the strongest threats to the regime. In fact, during the last years of the New State, education establishments were disturbed by growing agitation, and students were involved in different forms of conflictual activities: from those more connected to academic life – such as the occupation of university spaces – to more politicized and radical actions – such as support to deserters[1] and participation in actual terrorist activities. In other words, the future Portuguese political elites showed, during the last years of the New State, deep disaffection with respect to the regime in force.

Significantly, in defining this increasing unrest, the political police of the New State – the International and State Defence Police (Polícia Internacional de Defesa do Estado, PIDE), the future Directorate-General for Security (Direcção Geral de Segurança, DGS)[2] – began to use the emblematic expression of 'student effervescence'. To a certain extent, this institution, directed towards the control of social and political conflict in Portugal under the regime, suitably applied the concept of collective effervescence, penned by Durkheim almost a century previously. With this concept, the French sociologist indicated particular times during which new ideals and fresh visions of the world emerged from the collective which contributed to social change – 'magic' moments when individuals transcend themselves and prefigure a new collective order: 'In certain historical periods, social interactions become much more frequent and active. Individuals seek out one another and come together more. The result is the general effervescence that is characteristic of revolutionary or creative epochs ... People live differ-ently and more intensely than in normal times' (Durkheim 1995: 212–13).

It is important to emphasize that these moments, in the majority of cases, infringe the rules in force and act in the domain of illegality and, very often, that of criminality. However, Durkheim himself stresses that crime can contribute to social development, delineating the social values of the future. Normally, the acquisition of new rights or the process of aboli-tion of discriminatory rules follows this path of illegality to legality. This appears to be even truer if, as in the Portuguese case, crimes have been committed, especially political crimes, under authoritarian regimes. Hence, the social movements that emerge in moments of collective effervescence contribute not only to social change, but also to political and institutional change: social behaviour or political actions that are illegal thus impose their legitimacy and contribute to create new balances. From this perspective, it is interesting to note that PIDE/DGS identified the student effervescence as a particularly relevant risk to the fate of the New State. Indeed, Salazar's policy correctly recognized in this uprising the formation of new visions of the world and the potential to open new spaces of legitimacy, impose new behaviour, new forms of aggregation, which would have compromised the stability of the regime.

This awareness underpinned, especially as of the second half of the 1960s, the enormous effort of surveillance, constant and omnipresent, tow-ering over all activities at education establishments or linked to students. Detailed reports drawn up by informers or agents (of the PIDE/DGS or other police units) arrived at the Lisbon PIDE/DGS on a daily basis in the case of Lisbon, or weekly in the case of Porto and Coimbra. By the 1970s, student activism had become one of the most menacing threats to the regime, as demonstrated by the fact that in 1973 students numbered over half of all political prisoners.[3] This means that, by the end of the regime, stu-dents represented the social category most affected by the repression, which is even more significant considering that in Portuguese society this involved a fairly small group of people.

On the other hand, from the perspective of agents used to dealing with much more structured forms of opposition, the student effervescence, as its actual definition underlines, appeared from the onset to evade overly rigid categories and interpretations. The PIDE/DGS reflected on these difficulties right to the end, attempting to lead back the different student uprisings to defined ideologies, training or organizations. In reality, as will be shown, ideologies, training and organizations were changing from one day to another, above all as of the late 1960s. It was not only the regime that was inveighed with this wave of effervescence as the highest incarnation of authoritarianism, but also the historic organizations of the left.

In view of these considerations, the following pages seek to analyse the emergence, development and path of the Portuguese student contestation during the last two decades of the regime. Particular attention will be given to provide an in-depth examination of the role of student movements in the opening of democratic spaces under the New State, which presented a fundamental experience for the subsequent process of democratization. In this sense, the Portuguese student movement contributed to create an arena of participation and experimentation of social connections which, even more than the actual contents of the demands, were placed, in their horizontality, in clear contrast with the vertical dimension that the New State intended to imprint on civil society. At the same time, these forms of engagement and aggregation contributed to create some of the forms of participation that distinguished the revolutionary period that immediately followed the fall of the regime after the coup of 25 April 1974 – the so-called Processo Revolucionário em Curso (PREC, Revolutionary Process Underway).

The main part of this study covers the period between 1956 and 1974. The date of 1956 was chosen for two reasons. Firstly, this was the year that the Portuguese students' movement started to represent a specific and autonomous actor in the field of Portuguese contention against the New State. Moreover, 1956 was also an extremely important year at an international level, and especially in terms of social movements and conflictual politics. This will be explained in greater detail later, but for the moment I shall merely highlight two examples illustrative of the relevance of that year. On the one hand, 1956 was the year of the XX Congress of the Communist Party of the Soviet Union (CPSU), with Khrushchev's so-called 'Secret Speech', which had profound and broad-reaching consequences not only in the Eastern Bloc, but also in the ideologies, actions and agenda of Marxists all over the world, including Portugal. On the other hand, the two-year period of 1955–1956 was seminal in the development of the civil rights movement – mainly due to the famous 'Montgomery bus boycott' – and, consequently, for the subsequent movements that emerged around it, such as the American students' movement. As far as the date of 1974 is concerned, this was the year that the Portuguese dictatorship came to an end, followed by the Greek one a few months later, and then the Spanish regime in 1975. Moreover, at an international level, the mid-1970s can be situated as the end of the period that Arthur Marwick defined as the 'Long Sixties' (Marwick 1998), characterized by a transnational cycle of protest and radical change in the field of politics, culture and ways of life.

Politics in Movement: Students against Authority

As underlined by Kostis Kornetis for the Greek case (Kornetis 2013: 4), even if Marwick referred to democratic countries, and mainly Italy, France, Britain and the United States, this periodization can also be applied in the case of authoritarian states. The expression 'Long Sixties' refers, above all, to the cultural dynamics of the major changes that occurred during this period. However, the boundary lines between the social, cultural and political are always very blurred, as is demonstrated by the fact that the political authorities, in particular in authoritarian contexts, were always concerned in regulating the social and cultural behaviour of citizens, for example through censorship.

Undoubtedly, students were among the main actors of the Long Sixties all over the world: in Western liberal democracies, in the left-wing regimes of the Eastern Bloc, under the right-wing dictatorships of Southern Europe and Latin America, as well as in Maoist China. The common element of these large-scale and transnational student uprisings is in all certainty their anti-authoritarian tendency, whether against social and cultural behavioural models or against political institutions generally considered authoritative and conservative, albeit to different extents in different countries.

However, in the context of this work, I shall take into account, above all, the specifically political elements of the large-scale student mobilizations that spread all over Europe and many other parts of the world during the Long Sixties. On the one hand, while it is true that the movements that developed in authoritarian contexts – Eastern Europe, dictatorships of Southern Europe – were essentially directed at political change, it is also the case that in the movements that emerged in democratic regimes, in Europe and in the United States, the specifically political demands played a very important role. The actual democratic regimes were, in many cases, perceived by the student movements as having authoritarian characteristics, a perception that could be enhanced considerably by the effectively rather undemocratic response to the conflicts and social protests. On the other hand, various Western democracies showed, albeit to different degrees, effectively authoritarian aspects not only in the management of public order but also in the concession of fundamental rights, in terms of equal opportunities and in the steadfast existence of discrimination, endorsed or not by law, in relation to certain groups of citizens, such as for example, women, or, in the United States, the Afro-American community.

In this perspective, there is a line of continuity between the movements of the Long Sixties – the civil rights movement, colonial independence movements, student movements, feminist movements, to name but a few –

which is similar to the fight against the authoritarian aspects of the most diverse regimes and, in the case of Western democracies, to the stimulus towards compliance with promises made at the time of the democratization processes. In some cases, this democratization process was very recent. The example of Italy is significant in this case: the democratic transition, at the time of the first student movements in 1960, was only fifteen years old and the memories of fascism were still very alive. The great expectations of the democratization appeared to have been betrayed by the permanence of authoritarian elements, not only in political attitudes, but even in the actual legislation, whether civil or criminal. In this regard, as sensed, as Sidney Tarrow (1989) and della Porta and Reiter (2003) emphasize, from different points of view, the large-scale movements, in particular coming from students and workers of the Italian Long Sixties, played the role of providing new impetus to boost a democratization process that appeared to have become dormant, in particular in the areas of family law, education, labour legislation and in the management of public order.

The 'Long Sixties' under Authoritarian Rules

The recent literature dealing with aspects of transnational youth and student movements rightly stresses the need to look at this as a phenomenon that crosses national boundaries, although the nature of the movements varies according to local conditions (Klimke and Scharloth 2008; Klimke, Pekelder and Scharloth 2011; Kouki and Romanos 2011). As highlighted by Klimke, Pekelder and Scharloth, 'viewing the respective protests not only as parallel but interconnected phenomena on the global playing field of the Cold War' (2011: 20) is indeed important. However, while recent publications on the transnational wave of protest in Europe have addressed the cases of Spain and Greece, they lack any reference to the Portuguese movements, before or after the fall of the New State. Actually, the analysis of the Portuguese case might contribute to improving our knowledge of the contentious politics under the dictatorships of Southern Europe and their role in the subsequent democratization processes.

In the context of the Long Sixties, the case of the Portuguese student movement is thus particularly relevant for several reasons. First of all, as for other countries in Southern Europe, Portugal lived under an authoritarian right-wing regime during this entire period. As stressed before, this did not impede the development of social movements or the process of strong politicization and even radicalization among students and youth in general, which was in part similar to that occurring during these years in other countries living under different regimes. Nevertheless, it is obvious that the regime, besides limiting, to a great extent, the social and cultural changes that were taking place at an international level, in several ways conditioned the development of social protests, and, most importantly for this study, of student movements. On the other hand, with the fall of authoritarianism, the Portuguese – and likewise the Greek and Spanish – student movements and militants experienced a radical political, social and cultural opening. This opening had different and sometimes unpredictable consequences on student activism, the analysis of which – besides being important in itself – can also enlighten us on the processes of mobilization in authoritarian contexts.

The case of the student movement at the twilight of the Portuguese New State might thus allow us to better understand the possibilities of development, the perception of opportunities, and the claims and agenda of a social movement in the context of a right-wing dictatorship. The study might be also more fruitful if situated in the context of other analyses of student movements and the Long Sixties in authoritarian contexts, and mainly under the right-wing regimes of Southern Europe. Similar studies have started to see the light over recent years, such as the pioneering analysis by Kostis Kornetis (2013) on the Long Sixties in Greece, and the studies by Miguel Cardina and Giulia Strippoli on student contestation in Portugal, France and Italy (Cardina, 2008; Strippoli 2013). José Maria Maravall's monograph on student and worker opponents against Franco's regime, published back in 1978, while it did not situate the Spanish case in the larger context of the transnational mobilizations of the Long Sixties, also offers important reflections on this issue.

A common element that emerges in these studies is the predominance, in the student and youth movements of these countries, of political claims with respect to cultural and social demands. However, at least in Portugal, political claims only started to be at the centre of the student contestation as of the second half of the 1960s. Until then, even if political demands were certainly implied, the declared claims of the student activism were related to the students' condition and rights, and mainly to the defence of freedom of academic associations.

A further consideration must be made with regard to the repertoire of contention under an authoritarian regime (Davenport, Mueller and Johnston 2005; Tilly 2006). It is quite obvious that such a context radically moves the axis distinguishing legitimate and illegitimate actions. Most of the actions considered 'conventional' in a democratic context, being part of the normal process of political competition and participation, are usually considered illegal under authoritarian rules. All political activities developed beyond the regime's structures (such as the single party, or youth or women's organizations) are thus considered illegitimate. Creating or being a member of a political group or party – other than the regime's party – writing or disseminating a political flyer or journal, attending a political meeting or assembly, and many other activities considered normal and legitimate in a democracy, are illegal and, therefore, transgressive actions in most autocracies. Such actions, as occurred several times in the case of Portugal, could ultimately lead to imprisonment for political crime.

This pressure caused by illegality pushes political action and militants towards a clandestine dimension, which has strong effects on the form of political engagement and on the militants' biographies and trajectories in authoritarian contexts. In this sense, contentious political activism under dictatorships has a radically different significance than it does in democratic settings. As underlined by José Maria Maravall, with respect to student and worker activism against the late Franco's dictatorship:

> Three conditions in the process of becoming a dissenter have to be considered: the availability of radical ideologies, the commitment to such ideologies, and the conversion of this ideological commitment into political action. These three sequential steps in the process of political radicalization are determined by the existing political conditions, which act as restrictions on radicalism. These restrictions may be normative and non-normative, preventive and repressive. From this perspective, becoming a political dissident within a non-democratic context can be interpreted as a process similar to that of becoming deviant. (Maravall 1978: 118–19)

This also means that the costs of becoming a militant in an authoritarian context are far higher than in a democratic context. Among these costs, repression is a particular high one. The most evident form of repression is the 'direct' one, which is expressed in the control of public order, in violence against demonstrators, in the imprisonment of dissenters, in the absence of guaranties for the arrested, in the use of torture, and in the various kinds of security measures and forms of punishment for political crime. But there are also more 'indirect' forms of repression, such as making life difficult by impeding militants finding a job, carrying on their studies, developing social relations – and thus, because of their clandestinity, even starting a family. In any case, these high costs associated with becoming a dissenter also make it more difficult to step away from this condition and tend to increase the intensity of relations among militants. In this context, frequently the only possible exit – if one excludes the rare cases of dissenters who, more or less voluntarily, become collaborators of the regime, or exile – is their transfer from one group to another. In this sense, an authoritarian regime, such as the Portuguese one, might provoke a paradoxical 'absolutization' of political militancy. Thus, while the political demobilization of opponents is the main objective of such regimes, frequently they actually create a set of conditions that make the disengagement of the militants particularly difficult.

This mechanism can be observed from different points of view. Firstly, with respect to psychological costs, the high psychic costs borne for taking the identity of a dissenter in turn cause high costs to quit this same identity. From a material point of view, as seen above, the regime blocked almost all possible exits from political militancy – jobs, studies, relationships – which made their disengagement very complicated due to the difficulty for the militant to 'find a place' in society after leaving political activism.[4]

Returning to the case of the New State, it appears clear that, because political persecution meant imprisonment, exile, expulsion from university, a life in hiding and professional obstacles, for many anti-regime students – and militants in general – political engagement had entailed a radical discontinuity in life trajectories and, on the other hand, an intensification of the militancy's network (Accornero 2013a, 2013b and 2013c). When we look at these dynamics, we understand why, after the fall of the regime on 25 April 1974, most militants left political activity, or they decreased their engagement. The end of the dictatorship, besides introducing political freedoms, social and civil rights and a cultural renovation, also allowed political militants the possibility to restart the activities that they had been forced to abandon: the regime change opened up new educational, relational and professional avenues. This fact stresses, in contrast, the weight that the regime had on the opponents' trajectories of life.

Having said this, it is nevertheless necessary to consider that students represent a special category of militants, and this is especially true under an elitist and corporative regime such as the New State and in a hierarchical and vertical society such as Portugal's during the Long Sixties. In fact, the Portuguese academic milieu was, at least until the late 1960s, very restricted, and university students came from the most privileged sectors of society. Both due to their social origins and the special role that university played in the framework of the New State, students benefited from a series of advantageous conditions. Some of their rights, mainly in terms of freedom of association and participation, were unknown to most other citizens, and especially the other main actors of social conflict: the workers. As these rights had corporative legitimation, it allowed students to experience a space of participation unique in the context of the New State, as will be described in the following chapter.

Finally, another element that distinguishes and makes the case of authoritarian Portugal particularly significant for the analysis of student movements during the Long Sixties is the weight that the Colonial War had on the lives of people, especially youths and students. The Colonial War only entered the students' agenda as of the late 1960s, and mainly after a watershed demonstration in Lisbon in February 1968 against the Vietnam War, symbolically associated with the Portuguese war in Africa. Thereafter, the opposition to the war, combined with the claims against the dictatorship and the increasing demands for socialist solutions, strongly characterised the agenda, repertoire and aims of the Portuguese student movement under the late New State.

Indeed, in the final years of the regime, the more radical groups – mainly influenced by Maoism – were strongly critical not only of the dictatorship, but also, like their counterparts in other European countries, of the Western democratic model, which was criticized for being capitalist as well as authoritarian. The two processes of politicization before (started in the mid-1960s) and radicalization after (mainly as of the early 1970s) made the Portuguese student movement increasingly more similar, in terms of repertoire, agenda and claims, to the student movements in course throughout democratic Europe.

Portugal in Transitology

As is known, the Portuguese dictatorship ended with the famous Carnation Revolution. Not only was this a local event, but its resonance greatly transcended national boundaries. On the one hand, at a European level, the revolution was immediately regarded with enormous interest and hope by various Marxist groups, old and new, that had multiplied during the so-called Long Sixties. On the other hand, this event also represented a turning point in the field of political analysis on processes of change of regime.

Indeed, the coup d'état of 25 April 1974, put in motion by the Movimento das Forças Armadas (Armed Forces Movement, MFA) and through which Portugal was liberated in less than twenty hours from an authoritarian regime that had been in place for over forty years, inaugurated at an international level what would be defined as the 'third wave' of the democratization process (Huntington 1991). And it was precisely from this third wave – which apart from Portugal included Spain and Greece – that this area of political science, later to be called 'transitology', was conceived. In the words of one of its founders, Philippe Schimtter, 'The pretence of this neo- and, perhaps, pseudo-science is that it can explain and, hopefully, guide the way from one regime to another or, more specifically in the present context, from some form of autocracy to some form of democracy' (Schmitter 2014: 2).

Philippe Schmitter threw himself into studying the Portuguese case exclusively, based on which a large part of his theory of democratization would be developed. The monograph that he published, *Portugal do Autoritarismo à Democracia* (1999), was probably the first case study in the area of transitology entirely dedicated to Portugal, and represented a milestone not only for future studies on 25 April 1974, but also, at an international level, for the analysis of other cases.

The paradigm of 'transitology' was enormously successful during the 1990s, especially through the work published by Huntington and the famous work by Juan Linz and Alfred Stepan (1996). In their book, the authors produce a comparison of fifteen cases of democratic transitions in Europe and South America. The Portuguese case continues to be considered as 'unusual' with respect to all the other cases analysed, above all because of the cause of the 'crisis of the State' that followed the coup.[5]

Therefore, the first analyses of the Portuguese transition came to light in international studies of a comparative nature. These studies highlighted the unique aspects of the Portuguese transition when compared both to the Spanish and Greek transitions, and to the cases of Eastern Europe and South America. In fact, in the first place, the Portuguese process of democratization appeared to be characterized by elements of rupture that were much more profound than those that followed a few months later in Greece and Spain. This rupture was characterized by the actual way that the regime fell, through a peaceful military coup, and was extended by the major social mobilization that was triggered right after the coup, during the two years of the PREC (1974–1975). According to Thomas Bruneau, this Portuguese phenomenon was an 'unexpected transition' (Bruneau 1989). The developments of the military coup were considered unpredictable, above all because the embryonic beginning of a revolutionary transition process appeared to contradict the canons considered habitual in the case of military intervention in political life (Rezola 2010).

On the other hand, PREC was considered by various social scientists as a moment of exceptional social mobilization at a European level. Indeed, both the contemporary reports and the subsequent academic analyses, in most cases, also considered these mobilizations as rather unexpected. According to Manuel Braga da Cruz, this was an unprecedented mobilization with neither a past nor future in the history of the political attitudes of the Portuguese. In his opinion, the high levels of political participation by the Portuguese population during the revolution were a consequence of political and social decompression, the effect of which was a release of the accumulated tensions in society. However, he states that the subsequent demobilization showed that the deep-seated political culture of the Portuguese had remained unchanged (Braga da Cruz 1995). Likewise, Philippe Schmitter suggests that this phenomenon should be viewed as an 'awakening' of civil society, due to the institutional void produced by the coup d'état. This vision is shared by Howard Wiarda, who considers the political culture of the Portuguese as traditionally non-participative, with the exception of the transition period, when 'the "other Portugal" exploded in revolution' (Wiarda 2006: 123).

Thus, some of the most important studies on the Portuguese democratization process have portrayed elements of discontinuity among political participation and social mobilization during the transition, and among the levels of activism of the Portuguese before and after this moment. The social scientists who had addressed this issue were forced to face the challenge of explaining why there was this explosion of political and social participation, in its most diverse forms, during the PREC. In turn, my study seeks to demonstrate that the intense wave of mobilizations which characterized the Carnation Revolution did in fact have a past, and attempts to reconstruct, through particular focus on the student contestation, the processes that led to the 'unexpected' radicalization of the PREC. The analysis of social movements, more than a focus on institutional politics and processes led by political elites, can help, in my opinion, to throw light on this continuity. In this sense, I think that it is important to continue to look at the Portuguese case by analysing the long-term processes that led up to the great mobilization of the PREC, following the path opened by works such as *The Revolution within the Revolution* (Bermeo 1986) and *Building Popular Power* (Hammond 1988). Even if studies like these do not fit within that great area defined as 'sociology of social movements' – which is the main inspiration for my analysis approach, as I will explain below – they have been fundamental for understanding the bottom-up processes characterizing the Portuguese regime change, allowing an examination beyond the dominant elite-oriented approach.

Conducting Politics by Other Means

The historical reconstruction of the dynamics briefly described above will mainly be based on research developed in various Portuguese archives, especially the archives of the PIDE/DGS and of the Ministério do Interior (Home Office, MI), and on press sources, primarily the newspaper *Diário de Notícias* and student press and propaganda.[6] This empirical material has been analysed not only for the purpose of recreating the course of events, but also in order to understand the specificities of the profound dynamics that characterized the Portuguese student movement as a case of social movement developed under particular conditions – a right-wing regime and in a context of war – and during a special period – the Long Sixties. For such, the study has been developed with the support of different theoretical, methodological and analytical instruments.

While studies developed in the context of the so-called 'transitology' referred to above have been central in various analyses of the Portuguese change of regime, my main theoretical references come from the sociology of social movements. In fact, as stressed by Donatella della Porta, social movements 'during the different steps of the democratization process have rarely been addressed in a systematic and comparative way', and they 'have been far from prominent in the literature on democratization, which has mainly focused on either socioeconomic pre-conditions or elite behaviour'. Della Porta also stresses that, 'on the other hand, social movement scholars, until recently, have paid little attention to democratization processes, mostly concentrating their interest on democratic countries' (della Porta 2016: 53).

Following the implicit recommendation in these critiques, I thus attempted to apply the instruments developed by social movements studies in the analysis of the student mobilizations during the late Portuguese authoritarianism and the way in which they contributed to the transformation of a coup d'état into a revolution. As is well known, social movements studies address the forms of mobilization and militancy that are developed outside the official channels, and take on the characteristics of more or less open contestation to the institutional politics; the studies are on the borderline of different social sciences, such as political sociology, historical sociology and history. These less-conventional forms of conducting politics have been summarized under the name of 'contentious politics', which will frequently recur in this study.[7]

One of the key concepts that has been created in this context is that of Political Opportunity Structure (POS).[8] According to Sidney Tarrow's definition, political opportunities are 'consistent – but not necessarily formal, permanent or national – dimensions of the political environment which either encourage or discourage people from using collective action' (Tarrow 1998: 32). Some authors have also stressed the relevance of individual perception and networks' mediation in the interpretation of POS 'signals', while others have underlined the reciprocal interrelation between social movements and institutions, more than the unilateral influence of institutions on social movements.[9] These reinterpretations were strongly influential in the development of my study.

The first author to use the theoretical tools surrounding the concept of Political Opportunity to study the processes and possibilities of mobilization in Portugal was Rafael Duran Muñoz in his research on collective actions during the Spanish and Portuguese democratic transitions (Duran Muñoz 1997a, 1997b and 2000). Under these terms, Diego Palacios Cerezales (2003) conducted his study on the PREC which characterized the period after the fall of the New State. This author considers the great mobilizations characterizing this time to be a consequence of the opening of the POS following the coup d'état, which led to an actual crisis of the State.

Sidney Tarrow (1989) integrated the POS approach in a broader theoretical framework on the occasion of his study on the mobilizations in Italy between 1965 and 1975.[10] There he introduced also the concept of 'protest cycle', defined as 'a phase of heightened conflict and contention across the social system' involving, among others features, 'a rapid diffusion of collective action from more mobilized to less mobilized sector' (Tarrow 1998: 42). This last analytical instrument has been extremely helpful for interpreting the different phases of the Portuguese student movements and its progressive politicization and radicalization, two processes closely tied to two successive protest cycles that shook the country between 1956 and 1965, and between 1968 and 1975.

This study is thus structured to follow the evolution of these two protest cycles, and their relations with the changes that occurred in the New State itself. The first chapter highlights the relevance of the international events of 1956, with the Khrushchev report and Civil Rights Movements, in the scale of the contentious politics of the following years. Particular attention is also paid to the Sino-Soviet conflict, the China of Mao and the Cultural Revolution, which most catalysed the interest of the youngest militants – and also those living under right-wing regimes, such as the Portuguese – searching for new interpretations of Marxism and new forms to accomplish it. The field will be then restricted to focus on Portugal, to portray the existing student resources of mobilization in the context of the New State.

The second chapter focuses on the intense conflict that perturbed Portugal between 1958 and 1962, which had all the aspects of a cycle of protest. It would only draw to an end with the great wave of repression of 1964–1965, followed by a process of demobilization, pluralization of political forces, and radicalization. During this time, and until the end of the regime, students emerged as one of the main actors of the contentious politics in Portugal.

The third chapter starts with a description of the students' involvement in the relief provided to the population affected by the floods of 1967. This is a fine example of the fine tuning of mobilization resources and networks, and is considered as the starting point of a new protest cycle, whose path, however, would not be as linear as the first one, and in which the agitation at the University of Coimbra was to be particularly important. The fourth chapter deals with Marcelism, the last period of the New State characterized by the adoption of some measures of liberalization by the new Prime Minister, Marcelo Caetano, who replaced Salazar in 1968. It analyses the situation of the Portuguese academic milieu and especially that of Lisbon in the final years of the regime as one of permanent conflict, characterized by radical political atomization and polarization, the use of more transgressive and in some cases violent repertoires since 1968, and increasing distancing between the new and the old left wing. During this phase, the student movement increasingly resembles – in its ideologies, claims, repertoire and culture – the student and youth movements that were contemporaneously exploding in Europe.

The fifth and final chapter describes, on the one hand, the pluralization of the political forces on the eve of the revolution, and the increasing importance of the resistance to the Colonial War as a factor of mobilization and also as the main common denominator among the different opposition groups. The radicalization of the student movement and its shift to the new left, especially Marxist–Leninist, is thus followed until it merges in the protest cycle up to 1975.

Finally, one of the main aims of this volume is to stress the existing continuities among the mobilizations in course under the regime and against it, and in particular those led by students, and the social movements that characterized the PREC. As stressed above, a variety of social scientists such as Boaventura de Sousa Santos, Fernando Rosas and Pedro Ramos Pinto agree that the PREC was one of the periods of most intense mobilization in post-war Europe.[11] Various authors have analysed it in depth (Duran Muñoz 1997a, 1997b and 2000; Palacios Cerezales 2003; Ramos Pinto 2013), making a fundamental contribution to the study of the transitional period and mainly the PREC, from the point of view of social movements and contentious politics. On the other hand, except in the case of Ramos Pinto's work, also in these studies, contingent elements – such as the opening of the POS following the coup d'état – have generally been considered the key factors provoking this great wave of protest and participation.

The following pages will try to demonstrate that the explosion of social mobilizations characterizing the PREC had a recent past in the social movements – and in this case, mainly the student movement – developed in the fight against the New State. These mobilizations were themselves a strong factor contributing to the political opening. The 'revolution', before becoming a reality in Portugal during the two years of 1974–1975, had been a clear project strongly diffused among students and youth in general, and a powerful factor of mobilization against the dictatorship. With its innumerable undertones, from the more moderate to the more radical, this book would like to be the history of this project and of the fight carried on by Portuguese students to accomplish it.

Notes

1. As explained in the following chapters, Portugal was involved, from 1961 until the fall of the dictatorship in 1974, in a long and costly Colonial War against the independence movements in Angola, Guinea and Cape Verde. Opposition against the Colonial War was one of the main issues of student protests from the late 1960s until 1974.
2. Although the PIDE would only be transformed into the DGS at the end of 1968 (see Chapter 3 in this regard), the term PIDE/DGS will be used throughout herein, in order to standardize the text and facilitate its reading.
3. There were 187 student prisons recorded in 1973, with various students having been arrested more than once. In the same year, there were 289 prisons for other actors (source: Instituto dos Arquivos Nacionais Torre do Tombo – IAN/TT, Political Prisoners File of the PIDE/DGS).
4. These dynamics are well described by Olivier Fillieule, who stresses that 'the psychic or material cost of defection, and therefore its probability, is due to a number of factors amongst which we will mention the extent of the sacrifices accepted to enter the group (initiation rites, trials, hierarchization and isolation of collectives); weaker or stronger group socialization … and finally the rules in place at the time of the defection, sometimes rendered impossible by material dependence or the threat of being pursued as a traitor' (Fillieule 2010: 2).
5. However, according to Philippe Schmitter, the thirteen pages of Linz and Stepan's book dedicated to the Portuguese case 'ignore almost completely the issue of the dissolution of Portugal's overseas empire … What was more significant in the long run – and absolutely crucial for the eventual consolidation of democracy – was a dramatic and long overdue change in national identity, from an Atlanticist conception based on empire to one rooted in membership in the European Community' (Schmitter 1997: 168–74).
6. For a more exhaustive account of the sources used for this work, see the section 'Sources'.
7. One of the main authors to consider that contentious politics was not abnormal, but a source of social and political action of the same stature as other forms, was Charles Tilly, in particular in his pioneer essay *From Mobilization to Revolution* (1978), then subsequently in works that became classics such as *The Contentious French* (1986) and *European Revolutions, 1492–1992* (1993), and up to the most recent essay, co-authored with Sidney Tarrow, actually entitled *Contentious Politics* (2006). It is clear that in an authoritarian context, where the prospects of conducting politics through formal channels are very limited, any kind of opposition, whether partisan or not, finds its only possibility of expression in contentious politics.

8. Eisinger was the first author to use this expression in 1973 in order to explain the differences in the success of protests in different American cities, concluding that it depended, above all, on the degree of openness or rigidity of the local political systems (Eisinger 1973).
9. Doug McAdam, for instance, considers the emergence of social movements as 'a combination of expanding political opportunities and indigenous organization, as mediated through a crucial process of collective attribution' (McAdam 1999: 2). In turn, in his critique to the concept of political opportunities, Olivier Fillieule has shown that they are 'not structurally insensitive stocks that exist prior to action; rather, they are continuously updated through the relationship with the movements' (Fillieule 1997: 97).
10. It was in this study that the author delineated the concept of protest cycle, specifically identifying four relevant characteristics for the emergence of movements: (1) the level of openness/rigidity of formal channels of access to political power, (2) the stability/instability of political alignments, (3) the presence and strategic guidance of potential allies, and (4) the degree of division of the political elites (cf. Tarrow 1998: 42).
11. Boaventura de Sousa Santos defines it as 'the broadest, deepest people's social movement in post-war European history' (de Sousa Santos 1990: 27); Fernando Rosas as the 'last left-wing revolution in twentieth-century Europe' (Rosas 2004: 15); and Pedro Ramos Pinto as 'some of the widest popular mobilizations of post-war Europe' (Ramos Pinto 2007: iii).

Chapter 1

Two Decades That Shook the World: 1956–1974

Old Structures and New Conflicts

From Khrushchev to the New Left

The analysis of the Portuguese student movements throughout the 1960s and 1970s cannot ignore the formation of a left more to the left than the Communist Party which had, up until this date, represented the main reference point for the forces of opposition to the New State. In fact, the birth of a new left and its convergence with the student and youth movements was a common feature of the Western world as of the early 1960s, without major distinctions between the countries governed by authoritarian regimes and the democratic ones. Up to the end of the 1950s, in the imagery of militants and sympathizers of Western communist parties, the Soviet Union constituted, in fact, a symbol of hope in the actual achievement of an egalitarian society. In spite of this prestige, however, the accusations of excessive centralization and rigidity directed at Western communist parties, often coming from their own members, were not rare.

In this context, 1956 represents a fundamental year. The declarations of the new Secretary, Nikita Khrushchev, with the denouncement of Stalinism, at the XX Congress of the CPSU, had a profound effect on Western communist parties. The Soviet Union no longer represented socialist utopia while Western communist leaders were accused of having concealed and falsified the truth. The critique necessarily involved the actual inner functioning of parties as well as the attitude they maintained after the XX Congress.

On the other hand, the new course of the Soviet Union stipulated that Western communist parties should accompany 'the Soviet inflexions unhesitatingly' (Pacheco Pereira 2005: 345), inflexions that tended towards establishing a climate of 'peace in the world', correcting aspects that defined the sectarianism that had dominated the previous period. The interweaving between international and local elements emerges starkly at this point, since, while it may be true that the long waves of the XX Congress were a determi-

nant in the choices of Western communist parties, it is also necessary to highlight that they were inserted in dynamics specifically linked to the national
events of the 1950s. An example of such is the case of the Partido Comunista
Português (Portuguese Communist Party, PCP), whose main leaders, including Álvaro Cunhal, had been in prison since 1949. As demonstrated by one
of the principal researchers of the PCP, José Pacheco Pereira, this condition
led to a series of profound consequences in the history of the party over the
following years. Hence the effects of the Khrushchev era and of the successive,
and in part consequent, Sino-Soviet conflict, occurred under this scenario of
internal tensions, which found a provisional solution only in 1961, when, a
little after the Peniche prison escape of January 1960 and during the meeting of the Central Committee when he was appointed Secretary of the PCP,
Cunhal declared that it was necessary to suppress this tendency defined as
'anarcho-liberal' and responsible for a 'right-wing deviation'.

Knowledge of the critical situation of the party was hardly secondary
in determining the urgent need to escape from prison and embark on the
immediate restructuring of the party's guidelines. The new course was later
confirmed in 1965 during the VI Congress of the PCP held in Kiev, with
Álvaro Cunhal's presentation of the plan called *'Rumo à Vitória. As tarefas do
partido na revolução democrática e nacional'* ('Route to Victory. The Party's
tasks in the democratic and national revolution'), already discussed with the
Central Committee in 1964. This debate, in which the party was immersed
during the early 1960s, in the meantime coincided with the eclosion of
the Sino-Soviet conflict that hit the PCP at a critical moment of its history
(Pacheco Pereira 2008: 127). Thus, at the same time that the new Central
Committee of the PCP managed to re-establish a certain consensus within
the party in renewing objectives and strategies between 1963 and 1964, new
dissidence was sparked by the Sino-Soviet conflict and coagulated around
Francisco Martins Rodrigues, a member of the Executive Committee of the
Board. Having been imprisoned with Cunhal in Peniche and had escaped
with him in 1960, he was thus expelled from the party and founded the first
pro-Chinese organizations in Portugal, the Comité Marxista Leninista Português (Portuguese Marxist–Leninist Committee, CMLP) and the Frente
de Acção Popular (Popular Action Front, FAP).

These episodes will be explained in further detail below. At this stage,
it is sufficient to observe how the new strategy of political fight, of correc-
tion of the 'right-wing deviation' – theorized by Cunhal back in 1961 and
restated in 1965 – was not completely independent from this 'crossing over'
to the left by an explicitly revolutionary group which criticized the PCP,
above all, for its moderation and attitude of waiting. In fact, as shown by
Pacheco Pereira:

In the PCP's internal debate, the full revision of the 'right-wing deviation' line, which in many aspects represented Khrushchev's line after the XX Congress applied in Portugal, the substance of this rectification theoretically placed the PCP and Cunhal much closer to the Chinese theses than those of the Soviet approach. Cunhal was thus forced, at the same time as he fought against this tendency in Portugal as a 'right-wing deviation', to approve it as the line of the international communist movement. (Pacheco Pereira 2008: 128)

This sparked the beginning of this competition to the left which would lead, by the end of the decade, to the pulverization of the Marxist world and to the gradual loss of consensus of the PCP in the more radical wings of the opposition. Adopting Leninist language, Cunhal was to react to this situation, by now in 1970, accusing the 'leftists' of being 'renegades' and 'adventurers', especially due to the fact of not considering that the 'fight of the masses' was important to topple the regime and, therefore, of 'showing contempt for' the organization and political conduct aimed at creating consensus among the population (Cunhal 1970).[1]

The Soviet World and China

The most explosive consequences of the criticisms pointed at Stalinism by Khrushchev were immediately felt in Eastern Europe, above all in Hungary and Poland, where the report of the new Secretary of the CPSU gave rise to the illusion that the hegemony of the Soviet Union over its satellites could decline or even end completely. In Poland, it was in particular the workers supported by the Catholic Church who led the protests, which culminated in the great Poznań uprising in June 1956. The strike was suppressed by the intervention of Soviet troops, but the insurrection continued during the summer, having become a widespread movement of protest that extended to various sectors of society, which is now known as the Polish October. Instead of facing a difficult military repression, the leaders of the USSR decided to make a change in the vertices of the Polish party and government, favouring the rise to power of the former Secretary of the Polish Communist Party, Władysław Gomulka, who, imprisoned in 1951, had been rehabilitated following the XX Congress. Gomulka promoted a policy of cautious release of liberalization and partial reconciliation with the church, albeit never placing in question the alliance with the Soviet Union or the terms of the Warsaw Pact.

The far better known crisis in Hungary initially followed an almost analogous course, but culminated in a much more dramatic outcome. In this case, the leaders of the revolt were above all students and intellectuals, whose protests, during the month of October, ended in a real insurrection, also involving broad sectors of workers. Workers' committees autonomous of the official organizations were created in all factories. Imre Nagy, a communist of the liberal wing, who had already been expelled from the Communist Party, was called upon to head the government. When, on 1 November, Nagy announced the country's withdrawal from the Warsaw Pact, the Secretary of the Communist Party, Kadar, invoked Soviet intervention. Soviet Army troops occupied Budapest and violently repressed the resistance that had formed against them. A few months later, Nagy was executed, and Kadar took over the running of the country. The Soviet intervention, which appeared as a radical dashing of the hopes born of the de-Stalinization process, caused protests and denouncements at an international level, giving rise to real crises of conscience among communists all over the world, already affected by the trauma of the Khrushchev report.

Hence, while it is true that in the immediate term, concerning relations of force, the USSR managed to maintain control over its satellite states, it is also true that the experiences of Poland and above all Hungary marked the onset of a loss of consensus on the Soviet Union and the actually existing socialism among the weakest sectors of society, which had up to then always represented a model of the ideal society. On the other hand, the de-Stalinization was not only contested by the right wing, due to its betrayal of liberalizing promises, but also by the left wing, due to being considered a betrayal of the path designed by the fathers of communism, Marx, Engels, Lenin, Stalin and, finally, Mao. The factions that upheld this critique thus easily turned towards China, which began to represent the new model to be followed by the new Marxist–Leninist groups, composed especially by young people and students and, in Portugal, also by young deserters and conscientious objectors to military service in the Colonial War.

The Sino-Soviet conflict deepened these cleavages. This conflict was essentially based on State rivalry and political–ideological divergences, linked both to international strategies and internal politics. As emphasized by Pacheco Pereira: 'Both the CPSU and the CPC [Communist Party of China] were parties in power, commanding over countries with overlapping zones of influence, with distinctive national policies, each with their own particular weight in the communist movement, and each considered that they were entitled to define their own international policy' (Pacheco Pereira 2008: 10). Therefore, while the USSR proposed the maintenance of a bipolar world order, China contested the international status quo, in particular by supporting the cause of revolutionary movements all over the world, with the intention of representing a guiding model to developing countries against imperialism. Underlying this tendency was the Maoist idea that the revolution could be launched from countries of the third world; in other words, that a certain level of industrial development was not necessary for a revolution. It would be the rural masses, trained in guerrilla warfare, more than the proletariat, who would represent the fundamental actors of the revolution. This position – while it also showed evident motivations linked to its raison d'état, dictated by the interest in contrasting with the domain of the two superpowers (USA and USSR) and giving China a relevant role in the international context – had a deflagrating effect in the factious midst of Western Marxism, supplying an ideological baggage of the new utopias assumed and disclosed by the tiny Marxist–Leninist cells that began to sprout all over Europe. However, as shown above, while these dynamics exacerbated the process:

> The prehistory of the pro-Chinese and pro-Albanian groups in countries of Europe, America, Australia and New Zealand date from the XX Congress of the CPSU and of de-Stalinization, processes whose impact created tensions and resistance within communist parties ... These tensions led to dissidence of groups which evolved to other forms of communism, to the left and to the right, or to non-communist or radical socialist platforms, with progressive loss of communist identity. (Pacheco Pereira 2008: 65)

The Western World and May 1968

While in the Soviet world there was an opening of contestation of a liberalizing nature regarding the political and social structures of the existing socialism, in the Western world the contestation was in particular turned against capitalism and the inequalities that it was causing in the midst of the allegedly well-run welfare society. Moreover, as noted above, in more recently democratized countries, contestation was likewise directed against the authoritarian elements that also existed in democratic contexts, linked in particular to harsh measures in the management of public order and to aspects, endorsed or not, of social exclusion. The contestation of the capitalist model, not only economic but also cultural, embodied by the consumer society appeared initially, especially in the Anglo-Saxon world, under the guise of an absolute rejection of the industrialized society. This formed the underpinnings for the proliferation of hippy communities and later the creation of an alternative culture, into which flowed concepts such as conduct of non-violence, eastern religious philosophy, drug consumption and the messages of new music. Later, the youth insurrection would take on more politicized forms and find its driving centres at universities, where the education of the masses had given rise to a more numerous student body, and one that was more socially vociferous than ever before. Also in this case, the phenomenon began in the United States, where the mobilization – initiated with the occupation of the University of California, Berkeley in 1964 – was interwoven with the protests against the Vietnam War and the civil rights movement.

Following 1966–1967, and with its peak in 1968, the student uprising spread to Japan and the largest European countries, where it took on more radical and ideological forms. One of the principal unifying elements was, as we have seen, not only the fight against authoritarianism, considered to be a distinctive aspect of advanced industrial societies, but also the mobilization against 'American imperialism', especially against the intervention in Vietnam. In Germany, the student unrest was particularly concentrated against the repressive measures of the grand coalition government and against the major press, controlled by the right, giving rise to political organizations that defined themselves as extra-parliamentary. In France, the coagulation among the different movements of the extreme left, which sought to combine the traditional revolutionary fervour with new forms of anti-authoritarian fight, in line with the situationist movement, led to the most famous episodes of the entire season of student uprisings, those of May 1968.

The Italian Case and the Hot Autumn

Italian students had been at the genesis of an outbreak of mobilization back in 1960, when, together with various sectors of workers, they contested the formation of a single-colour Christian-Democrat government which had the external support of the Movimento Sociale Italiano (Italian Social Movement, MSI), a party that was the direct heir of fascism and up to this time officially excluded from the political arena. Merely fifteen years after the end of the regime, this choice was considered offensive to the new democratic institutions and a betrayal of the constitutional values expressed by all the forces that had participated in the resistance fight. The protests that emerged were violently repressed, and nine young students, all aged between 18 and 21, were shot dead by the police during the demonstrations. The student protests resurged in Italy particularly from 1967 onwards, leading, in this case, to the occupation of numerous universities and to major demonstrations in the streets, as well as, once again, violent confrontations with the police.

At this stage, the Italian uprising incorporated issues that were already present in the movements of other countries (anti-imperialism, opposition to the Vietnam War, anti-authoritarianism, anti-capitalism), but also showed specific characteristics in terms of a strong Marxist and revolutionary ideological basis, rooted firmly in the 'workerist' tradition. The student movement grew in the fight against academic authoritarianism and the principle of school selection, but assumed an increasingly more hostile opposition in relation to the entire capitalist system and bourgeois culture in general (Ortoleva 1988; Agosti, Tranfaglia and Passerini 1991). The criticism levied at the bourgeois society was transformed into a rejection of traditional political conduct, including historical left-wing parties, the exaltation of grassroots democracy based on collective decision making and egalitarianism. This search for new forms of conducting politics was accompanied, in many cases, by a revolution in sexual behaviour, and in personal and family relations.

Following the autumn of 1968, the student movement identified the proletariat as its preferred and target partner. The search for this connection derived not only from the influence of the intellectual groups which had for some time assumed workerist positions, but also, more generally, from the presence of a strong Marxist tradition which had characterized the culture of the Italian left throughout the entire post-war period. Workerism was also a distinctive feature of the political groups that emerged between 1968 and 1970 in the wave of the student movement, and that, as in the German case, began to call themselves extra-parliamentary. Among other cases, we recall the 'Potere Operaio' (Workers' Power), 'Lotta Continua' (Continuous Struggle) and 'Avanguardia Operaia' (Workers' Vanguard) (Grandi 2003; Cazzullo 2006).

The attention given to the working classes by Italian students coincided with an intensive period of struggle by industrial workers which, having started in early 1969 on the occasion of a series of contractual renewals, culminated in the autumn of that year. The protest had begun almost spontaneously in various large factories in the north, with its main protagonist being the figure of the so-called mass worker – in other words, the unqualified worker, often an immigrant from the south and, therefore, upon whose shoulders the working conditions and lack of adequate social services weighed most heavily. On the other hand, while in many cases the workers from the north already had a strongly structured political education given by the Confederazione Generale Italiana del Lavoro (Italian General Confederation of Labour, CGIL) and very often by the Partido Comunista Italiano (Italian Communist Party, PCI), which made radicalization more difficult, the workers from the south represented virgin territory to a certain extent for the recruitment of militants in the organizations of the extreme left. Through the influence of the student uprising, these conflicts in companies were characterized by the use of the repertoire of the general meeting as the decision-making moment, due to the high level of participation and the radical nature of the demands, focused on egalitarianism (such as equal wage increases) and in the contestation of the organization of work in the factories.

In spite of these results of the groups of students and the new left wing in terms of conducting the workers' movement, the traditional union organizations managed to lead the direction of the fights and guide them towards the conclusion of a series of national contracts that in some cases assured significant wage increases. Finally, the new power wielded by the unions was demonstrated by the adoption, in 1970, of the first Statute of the Workers, which established the union freedoms and the rights of workers within companies. However, this led to the widespread demobilization of the majority of the workers who were satisfied with the achieved results, while the more politicized workers, together with the more radical factions of the student movement and new left-wing groups, felt increasingly more isolated, venturing down the road of violent confrontation and, finally, terrorism.

On the other hand, the student and workers' insurrections found few possibilities to affect a political system that revealed, on that occasion, all its rigidity, low level of dynamism and more authoritarian facets, which were expressed above all in the violent repression of the movements. The only relevant intervention in the area of education was the liberalization of access to university which, however, was not accompanied, as it should have been, by a simultaneous reform of secondary school education or of the actual higher education system. Notwithstanding this, and although the changes were not exactly as radical as had been intended by the students, various important laws were passed during those years that were aimed at profoundly affecting Italian institutions and society. Apart from the Statute of the Workers referred to above, whose importance is irrefutable, in 1970, for example, measures were adopted to decentralize power, through the institution of regions. In the same year, with the support of the left-wing and secular political parties, the Fortuna-Bastini law was approved, which introduced the right to divorce in Italy. Along these lines, the first reform of family rights since the fascist epoch arrived in 1975, with important measures aimed at equality between men and women, while abortion was finally decriminalized in 1978 (Ungari 2002).

Student Networks and Repertoires under the New State

The New State: A 'Border Fascism'[2]

While the world was being shaken by these episodes, Portugal still lived partially frozen under a regime that was a relic of times gone by. The Portuguese New State was a corporate authoritarian regime born during the period of European fascisms, but which survived the fall of Mussolini and Hitler until 1974. In 1926, the First Portuguese Parliamentary Republic, founded in 1911, had been slain by a coup d'état that had implemented a military dictatorship. António de Oliveira Salazar, who had been Minister of Finance of this dictatorship since 1928, was appointed President of the Council in 1932; and, in 1933, through a plebiscitarian vote in favour of the New Constitution, he founded the regime of the New State. He thus became the absolute head of this regime until 1968, when he was replaced, due to health reasons, by Marcelo Caetano.

The New State essentially drew its inspiration from Italian Fascism, albeit with substantial specificities, such as the strong influence of the social doctrine of the Catholic Church and the absence of expansionary policies, due to the fact that Portugal already had a large colonial empire (Adinolfi 2007; Accornero and Adinolfi 2014). The New State most determinedly adopted the principles of fascist corporatism in the social and economic sphere, on the one hand, and in the management of public order and control of political dissidents, on the other.[3] In 1930, the then Minister of Finance, Salazar, announced the creation of a single party, the União Nacional (National Union, UN). Quite differently from the Italian or German case, this single party was not an instrument for the conquest of power, but, created afterwards, was used to maintain and consolidate the new regime, successively endorsed by the Constitution. With this, the different institutional bodies that existed up to 1974 were created. The chamber of members of parliament was renamed the 'Assembleia Nacional' (National Assembly, AN), and, elected through majority direct suffrage,[4] had official legislative powers, but no power of supervision of the government's activity, which depended exclusively on the Head of State. In the meantime, legislative activity was seldom exercised, so it can be said that the AN was never more than a chamber of resonance for the regime. The Corporate Chamber was created alongside the AN, 'composed of representatives of local government and social interests, the latter considered in their fundamental domains of administrative order, cultural ethics and economic issues' (article 102), entrusted with merely advisory duties.

As is the case of all regimes, the New State was also based on two complementary processes: the mobilization of consensus and the repression of opposition (Morlino 2003). A particularly important aspect of the first process was the constitution of the Secretariado da Propaganda Nacional (National Propaganda Secretariat, SPN) – created in 1934 and replaced in 1945 by the Secretariado Nacional da Informação (National Information Service, SNI) – and, simultaneously, the institution of prior censorship. Moreover, the regime created a youth organization – the Mocidade

Portuguesa (Portuguese Youth, MP) – membership to which was compulsory between the ages of 7 and 14, and then voluntary until the age of 25. Founded in 1936, it was originally inspired by the model of the Italian Fascist 'Opera Nazionale Balilla' and the Nazi Hitler Youth. However, in 1940 the Germanophile National Secretary Francisco Nobre Guedes was replaced by the Anglophile Marcelo Caetano, who gave the organization a different orientation, withdrawing from the Hitler Youth and abandoning its paramilitary feature, and instead approaching the Catholic Church and youth organizations such as the Scout Movement (Vieira 2008).

Repression was one of the areas in which the New State most diligently applied the model of other European fascisms. In 1933, Salazar directly ordered the creation of the Polícia de Vigilância e Defesa do Estado (Surveillance and State Defence Police, PVDE),[5] entrusted above all with controlling political crime, and strongly inspired by the OVRA, the Italian Fascist secret police.[6] In 1945, the political police was renamed the PIDE. The objective of this change was to give the appearance of being closer to the secret services of the Western democracies. Because, with the end of the Second World War and the defeat of the main European fascisms, and with Portugal's prospective joining of NATO in 1948, it would have been very difficult to justify the maintenance of a political police force (Flunser Pimentel 2007). A text was published in 1933 which was considered as a founding block of the regime's political repression: Decree-Law 23 203 of 6 November. This legislation identifies political crimes in, among others: propaganda, incitement or any means of provocation to social discipline, and violent subversion of the institutions and fundamental principles of society.

These crimes were punishable by a sentence of deportation, prison or fines. The competent court for political trials was a special court; that is, a military court which had been vested with this competence by the government (since 5 September 1936, through Decree-Law 26 981).[7] What was built, in fact, was a special system for the purpose of the definition, control and repression of political crime, whose procedural path should be completely different from that of common crime. The first concentration camp was created in Angola in 1934. However, the most – grievously – known concentration camp was that of Tarrafal, in Cape Verde, which, closed in 1956, would be reopened in 1970 in order to relegate prisoners of the independence movements of the African colonies. Article 2 of Decree-Law 26 539, of 23 April 1936, stipulated that Tarrafal camp was intended for 'political and social prisoners, on whom it befell the duty to comply with deportation, or those imprisoned in other prison establishments who showed resistance to discipline as well as those who were pernicious to other prisoners'.

The regime also established prisons specifically for political criminals: Aljube prison, in Lisbon, which was closed in 1965; Caxias prison, between Lisbon and Cascais; the Porto PVDE prison; and Peniche prison, intended only for men and compliance with security measures – in other words, a system of extensions of the sentence for two-year periods until '[t]he prisoner showed aptitude to lead an honest life'.[8] After a major wave of social unrest in 1934, the National Assembly approved a law on secret societies (Law 191 of 21 May 1935). The Constitution did not prohibit associations of citizens, except secret associations. With the new rules, the concept of a secret association was given a much broader definition, including not only groups that developed clandestine activities, but also those whose leaders refused to provide the authorities with details of their activities, composition, statutes, and identification of members. Lastly, civil servants were obliged to sign documents on which they declared that they did not belong to a secret society. In 1936, in particular due to the need to channel the most radical souls at the roots of the regime (such as, for example, the current of Lusitan Integralism inspired by Maurras) and increase surveillance as a result of the Spanish Civil War, Salazar instituted the Legião Portuguesa (Portuguese Legion, LP), a voluntary militia with the duty to 'defend the spiritual heritage of the nation and combat the communist and anarchist threat'.[9]

Finally, it is important to refer to other policies that already existed before the implantation of the regime and which had been the main forces of repression during the Parliamentary Republic: the Polícia Judiciária (Judicial Police, PJ), dependent on the Ministry of Justice; the Polícia de Segurança Pública (Public Security Police, PSP), dependent on the Ministry of the Interior; and the Guarda Nacional Republicana (National Republican Guard, GNR), a body similar to the French *gendarmerie* and Italian *carabinieri*, dependent on the Ministry of the Interior and the Ministry of Defence. While the PIDE performed a primarily investigational role, the PSP and GNR were the main forces of control of public order and of repression of the public protests in Portugal, the former in urban areas and the latter in rural areas.

Another area where the regime soon intervened was that of labour and the regulation of relations between the different social forces. The underlying objective of this effort was primarily to eliminate any embryonic sign of social conflict, since this very conflict was seen as the worst evil that could befall a corporate and organic State. With regard to the organizations of the defence of workers' interests, Maria Fátima Patriarca emphasizes that the National Syndicates, in which the government had imposed compulsory enrolment through decree in 1939, were transformed with the arrival of Salazarism into an 'emanation of the State' (Patriarca 1995: 224), responding primarily to the requirement that 'the coordination and development of the national economy should be part of the political organization' (ibid.: 220).

Indeed, apart from being under close and constant political control, these institutions became entities aimed at sublimating the conflicts between workers and their masters in a specifically corporate perspective which excluded the possibility of class struggle. This corporatization of the syndicates had been imprinted by the regime, ever since its implementation, through the adoption of legislative measures that strongly limited their independence and duties. Hence, for example, Decree-Law 23 050 established that: 'The syndicates obey three fundamental principles: that of the hierarchy of interests, which subordinates individual interests to those of the national economy; that of collaboration with the state and other classes; and that of nationalism, which limits syndicate activity exclusively to the national sphere, in absolute observance of the higher interests of the nation' (Patriarca 1995: 228).

At the same time the new legislation determined that the statutes of the syndicates should contain, in addition to the 'expression of loyalty to nationalism and social collaboration', a declaration of renouncement 'of all and any activity contrary to the interests of the Portuguese nation and the repudiation of the class struggle' (Patriarca 1995: 228). Also very important were the articles that attributed only to the government the power to sanction the selection of senior staff, whose election by the members was only valid after the approval of the Under Secretary of State for the Corporations. This legislation did not fall on neutral and perfectly mouldable matter, but rather gave rise to an 'amalgam which resulted from the confluence of the principles defined by the legislation, the more or less orthodox interpretations' and resistance of the pre-existing organizations (Patriarca 2004: 293). However, as shown by Philippe Schmitter, in spite of the ambiguities and weaknesses of this process, the corporate institutions and primarily the syndicates were able to play an important role, not so much in terms of representing economic interests, but rather in 'filling a political space', and thus preventing the emergence of 'alternative forms of collective action' (Schmitter 1999: 13).

Student Associativism

As has been seen, therefore, the consented space for organized collective action, especially of the associative type, was subject to the important variations during the enforcement of the New State. As in the case of censorship (Adinolfi 2007), the authorities actually modulated their repressive action against associativism according to the demands of the time, albeit always within the limits of close control. The free associativism of citizens was legitimated, in principle, by the actual Constitution 1933, which only barred the formation of secret associations. However, the association and meeting of citizens was also persecuted in Salazarist Portugal as a potential instrument of subversion and disturbance of public order. This was, on the other hand, by the institutions, an attitude that was absolutely in conformity with the basic principles of the organic State, where all members of the national body should be interdependent and linked in a hierarchical manner. From this point of view, the formation of autonomous associations, constituted based on individual voluntarism and on a type of social relations with horizontal characteristics, openly clashed with the vertical and authoritarian structure of the State.

The student associations partially escaped from these dynamics, particularly due to being corporate bodies – with strong elitist features – and, in fact, very structured inside the universities, even if they frequently turned into environments of insubordination to the regime. It was precisely here that there was a partial contradiction for the student associations: although they were official centres of aggregation and linked to a tradition that was, in some cases, not exactly progressive, they represented, through their actual characteristics, very favourable environments for the coagulation of dissidence. The principal factor underlying this capacity resided in the fact that student associations were one of the few places that were effectively self-managed under the regime. Through the associations, the students were provided with an effective and independent instrument of representation, whereas nothing even vaguely similar existed for other social categories, especially the workers.

As will be shown further below, in 1956 the government attempted, through the preparation of Decree-Law 40 900, to institute similar rules to those established for the syndicates to regulate the life of the student associations and place the election of the students' representatives under the close control of the State. Although this legislation was not approved, also thanks to the student unrest which blocked its sanction, the government managed its affirmation subsequently with Decree-Law 44 632, adopted after the academic crisis of 1962. However, its effective application, which the student associations endeavoured to resist, was always very problematic, and represented one of the principal elements of conflict between students and authorities.

This situation implied that the student associations were to emerge as a partial exception: in addition to their specific mission to defend the interests of the students, their structure was also rather unusual and potentially destabilizing for the New State, above all due to the particular form of its decision-making process which involved general meetings open to all students of all courses, and which were considered the 'the highest deliberative body'.[10] The executive power of the student associations was, in turn, held by the General Board, elected through 'secret and individual universal vote', which also had the competence, albeit not exclusive, to call the general meeting.[11]

Especially as of the 1950s, the activism of these bodies started to expand towards involvement in issues directly linked to the regime's policy, first concentrating on topics of a specifically educational nature and later beginning to consider the wider dimension of the authoritarian nature of the regime. In less than a decade, the associations had become one of the most important centres of criticism and dissent, and even constituted a fundamental network of organization and mobilization for action against the regime, and no longer only by students. At the same time, the relative autonomy of the associations began to be questioned by the government and this increased the concern and control exerted by the forces of public order, which, while they had tried to control this space from 1956 onwards with the promulgation of legislation limiting their autonomy, as of the second half of the 1960s the authorities began to infiltrate the associations with a dense network of informers.

By the end of the 1960s and early 1970s, and simultaneously with the process of radicalization of some sectors of the student movement around the student associations, various groups of the radical left were formed, in particular Marxist–Leninist ones. The associations provided not only essential material resources and logistics for the creation and development of these groups – such as, for example, meeting places and copygraphs – but also, being in the main centres of student aggregation, also conveyed exceptional human and ideological resources. At the same time, in many cases, supported by groups of the radical left, they managed to win academic elections and occupy the General Board. In this last case, it is natural that a major part of association activity would be channelled in a specifically political direction along the lines of the majority group, and that the news bulletin of this university would also become an instrument of propaganda.

Therefore, student activism coagulated around the student associations, developing in different forms and ways over time. The strategy of the PCP, for example, was to keep these two spheres of action very separate: the legal, characterized by conventional and not openly conflictual actions, which might involve the majority of the students, and the illegal, which would be developed exclusively in a conspiratorial form, by clandestine militants. The groups of the new left which spread above all in the late 1960s, considered, to the contrary, that it would be more opportune not to draw a radical line between the two spheres, separating them, and that it was necessary to adopt frontal and explicitly conflictual strategies of opposition immediately through legal bodies, such as student associations.

Throughout the entire 1950s, the academic associations had consistently expanded their weight and influence. While, in a general manner, this phase is considered as rather non-politicized, in fact the management of academic life and its spaces implied a series of problematic issues and choices that had all the characteristics of conducting politics. For example, the largest academic association of Lisbon, the Instituto Superior Técnico (Higher Technology Institute, IST), substantially managed all the extracurricular activities that were carried out in the most diverse sections: pedagogy, press, social, economic, medical, cultural, library-related, photographic, sports and international. At an inter-university level, there was also a body that coordinated the activities of the associations of the different institutes, named Comissão Inter Associações (Inter-Association Commission, CIA) between 1949 and 1954, and Reuniões Inter Associações (Inter-Association Meeting, RIA) since 1954. Although little of this emerged through the official press, the authorities were fairly concerned with this activism, especially because, apart from being accomplished in a conventional manner in the management of normal academic, cultural and recreational activities, it had already portrayed certain hostility towards the government's close control of education establishments. This hostility had arisen on occasions after 1952, when a great action day against the Atlantic Pact was organized in Lisbon, especially by student leaders of the Faculty of Medicine and the IST. The underlying ideological motivation of the protest – in other words, the objection to nuclear proliferation and the Cold War – was inscribed in a more specific context of the defence of student space, since the very premises of IST were intended to host the meeting of the Council of the Atlantic Pact, with the consequent suspension of classes and exams.

Managing to escape from the close police control, students of the IST, supported by colleagues from other colleges, covered the walls of this establishment with pacifist slogans against nuclear proliferation and against fascism. While, on the one hand, this action led to the imprisonment of many students of the different Portuguese higher education system establishments, it should be emphasized that, in fact, it achieved the objective of preventing the suspension of exams and the interdiction of the premises to the students, forcing the government to open a provisional entrance. The success of the action was also highlighted by the PCP news bulletin, *Avante!*, which, in the February 1952 number referred to 'a clear victory' for the students 'of all academic years and courses, adopting the most varied political tendencies and religious beliefs'.[12]

This and other examples of insubordination demonstrate how the calm Portuguese 1950s – known as the 'gloomy years' (*anos de chumbo*) – were, in reality, imbued with more or less latent conflicts between students and authorities, as well as frequent waves of repression. In 1953, for example, the government decreed the closing and dissolution of the Associação de Estudantes da Faculdade de Medicina de Lisboa (Student Association of the Faculty of Medicine of Lisbon, AEFML), which, together with the Student Association of the IST, had led the protest of February 1952. The same fate befell the Associação de Estudantes da Escola Superior de Belas Artes do Porto (Student Association of the Academy of Fine Arts of Porto, AEES-BAP) in 1955.

The common thread of the student protests of these years continued to be the opposition to the Atlantic-based choice of Portugal – which had belonged to the Atlantic Pact since 1949 – and, indeed, nuclear proliferation. As the press highlighted in 1953, over one hundred young pacifists were imprisoned, mostly in Porto and in the north of the country, of whom fifty-five were taken to trial and thirty were sentenced two years later. On this issue, the words of Salazar in a letter to the President of the Republic, Craveiro Lopes, are significant:

> Over recent times, the police force has shown its concern on the very intense catchment of students by communist organizations. Boys and girls from the best families, both in terms of wealth and moral education, appear trapped in these organizations ... And the worst is that they show such factiousness that any conversion or hope of conversion seems lost. This is a very serious case which is difficult to overturn by police means alone, where an ideological counteroffensive becomes necessary. (Lourenço, Costa and Pena 2001: 16)

The Youth Democratic Unity Movement

The generalized Salazarist expression of 'communist organizations' in reality refers to the Movimento de Unidade Democrática Juvenil (Youth Democratic Unity Movement, MUDJ), which was widespread in Portuguese universities from the end of the 1940s until the end of the following decade. The MUDJ had been founded on 28 June 1946, particularly by the initiative of the PCP, and replaced the youth organization of this party that had been active up to this time: the Federação Juvenil Comunista Portuguesa (Portuguese Communist Youth Federation, FJCP). This represented an initiative coherent with the anti-fascist unity strategy of the last years of the Second World War, and had already led to the creation, in 1945, of the Movimento de Unidade Democrática (Democratic Unity Movement, MUD), tolerated by the government initially but later made illegal in 1948.

The MUDJ inherited the majority of its leaders from the FJCP, and the Central Committee was composed of figures destined to play extremely important political roles in the country's fate, such as the future founder of the Partido Socialista (Socialist Party, PS) and future President of the Republic, Mário Soares. Underlying this initiative was the determination to gather together all the student and youth opposition under a single banner, which was not directly linked to socialist-type demands. Hence, the appeal to a more general fight against the dictatorship, for rights and peace, was the outcome of a strategic choice made by the PCP to achieve penetration in university environments, where the FJCP appeared to have an overly restricted base.

With this decision, the PCP waived any direct youth emanation at least until 1979, when the Juventude Comunista Portuguesa (Portuguese Communist Youth, JCP) was founded. Although it rapidly became the target of Salazarist repression, with all the members of the Central Committee since 1947 having a personal file in the archives of the PIDE/DGS, and with dozens of people imprisoned, the MUDJ was a winning choice. From its very first years of existence, the organization had over two thousand enrolled members and, until it was made illegal in 1957, it carried forward a constant struggle in terms of creating a space of legal and semi-legal participation. From the start, the MUDJ operated to become the centre of stimulation of student opposition, through a specific programme for the university sector. For example, for the summer vacation period 1947, a 'stimulation plan' was implemented, so as 'not to lose contact with the students'.[13] This plan established fraternization sections to connect university students to the MUDJ, and 'preventing infiltrations through reactionary girls'.[14] For this purpose, it was requested 'that all members of secondary schools and colleges provide indication of reactionary students, including their courses and addresses'.[15] Later, 'camaraderie on the beach and spas [was organized] with all members of secondary schools and study meetings always outside cities and with no more than four to five people, taking special care of the doctrinal orientation towards the university fight'.[16] This should take into account the party's framework for the inclusion of boys and girls, 'endowing them with a mentality of greater liberty in relations of comradeship with a democratic spirit'.[17]

In 1952, the MUDJ drew up a national text against the Atlantic Pact signed by thousands of people, young or not, intellectuals, artists, teachers, doctors and lawyers, as well as some members of the future liberation movements of the colonies. Pacifism and opposition to nuclear proliferation were, in fact, very heartfelt issues at that time – and not only in political environments – and it was around these issues that the MUDJ based a large part of its campaigns throughout the 1950s, such as the protest that involved the main academies of Lisbon in 1952. Illegalized in 1957 and surviving underground for a further year, the student contestation of 1956, the first widespread student fight against the government, was the last battle fostered and coordinated through the MUDJ. The organization was later dissolved, however, leaving a notable contribution in terms of mobilization networks and repertoire, which would have increasingly more frequent occasions to become active over the following years.

Catholic Organizations

However, the MUDJ was not the only youth organization around which student discontent simmered, since, also in the Catholic context, there began to be at this time a certain distancing from the situationist positions. The two principal Catholic academic organizations were the Juventude Universitária Católica (Catholic University Youth, JUC) and, in Coimbra, the Centro Académico de Democracia Cristã (Christian Democracy Academic Centre, CADC). Until 1953, the leaders of the JUC showed an attitude of conformity with the government, as was evident in the I National Congress, when a young student denounced the attempt 'of certain factions' to dominate the student associations in order to lead them to struggles beyond the interests of the students. The line coming out of the congress was, therefore, that of requesting greater activism by Catholic students in order to counter these 'certain factions', an expression that in fact indicated the members of the MUDJ.

Although it is difficult to reduce the phenomenon to the decisions taken at I Congress, over the following years there was in fact a higher participation by Catholic students in the academic associations. However, as frequently occurs, this participation very soon transcended its initial purposes and contributed to drawing various members of the JUC closer to more critical positions in relation to the regime. This turnaround gained most strength from 1956 onwards, when members of the Catholic organization, such as Carlos Portas, associative leader of the Faculty of Agronomy, and João Benard da Costa, leader of the Faculty of Letters, joined the student contestation against Decree-Law 40 900, in open controversy with the senior ranks of the JUC. Indeed, this fact was merely the first sign of a process through which the JUC moved definitively away from the government, having become an important canal for the organization of student conflict.

The CADC – the organization in which Salazar himself had taken his first political steps – had actually taken up critical positions in relation to the regime at an earlier stage, that is, in 1949, when the president of the organization, Orlando de Carvalho, had supported General Norton de Matos, a candidate of the opposition, in the presidential elections. The CADC also adopted a more interventionist attitude in university politics around 1953, when the organization's magazine, *Estudos*, started to dedicate more attention to the students' social problems, especially regarding accommodation, medical care and associative activities. In 1956, together with colleagues from the JUC, the leaders of the CADC organized a day of solidarity with the young students and workers of Hungary. This was actually an experience of mobilization and participation that, while supported and even requested by the regime, would play an important role a few months later in these organizations joining the movement of objection against Decree-Law 40 900 – that is, against 'too much interference of the State in the free association of individuals and consequently also in academic bodies, since this creates deforming and etiolating paternalism'.[18]

The Film Society Movement

Another fundamental circuit in the process of mobilization of university contestation was the film society movement, which not only served as a specific logistical resource but also as a vehicle of a culture – and an ideology – that was alternative and ultimately subversive in relation to that imposed by the regime. As demonstrated by Paulo Jorge Granja concerning the situation of culture linked to the cinema during the post-war era, 'the environment was small and journalists and critics frequently showed interest in the cinema world, with the film reviews being more independent due to being developed in literary and cultural seminars and publications, almost always to the left of the regime, such as for example *O Globo, Seara Nova* and *O Diabo, Vértice*' (Granja 2002: 29–30).

It was in this context that the first Portuguese film societies emerged. As in the rest of Europe, they were above all Marxist orientated, a tendency that deepened with the Cold War through close adherence to the precepts of socialist realism. Hence, the film societies also began to 'play an important role in ideological combat through the cinema'. In this context, the Clube Português de Cinematografia was founded in 1945 in Porto, followed in 1947 by the Círculo de Cinema de Lisboa and the Círculo de Cultura Cinematográfica de Coimbra.

Although they could not compete, in terms of audience, with the commercial cinemas, the film societies made a notable contribution not only at a cultural level, but also at an ideological and political level. The same can be said of the actual film reviews, which were disseminated especially through newspapers such as *Diário de Lisboa*, mainly in the cultural pages, or in specialized magazines such as *Imagem* and *ABC*. It was not so rare for cinematographic analysis to involve, in a more or less explicit form, a critique of the political situation or the affirmation of an ideological position, in particular because the borderline between alternative culture and political insubordination was rather murky. The pages of these magazines frequently included the writings of figures of the opposition, who were often fiercely critical of the official Portuguese cinema, hence 'it is hardly strange that in 1952 the critic of the national broadcasting station Emissora Nacional, Domingos Mascarenhas, spoke of certain political tendencies portrayed in the pages of the magazine *Imagem* in perfect synchrony with a well-known general line which has Moscow at one point and the moon at the other' (Granja 2002: 31–32). The Cineclube ABC and Cineclube Imagem were created in 1951 in Lisbon, linked to their homonymous magazines; Cineclube Universitário de Lisboa was founded in 1952 and, while still at this time closer to the regime, Cineclube de Rio Maior, linked to the magazine *Visor*.

Finally, there was a real explosion of the phenomenon from 1954 onwards, with the appearance of twenty such entities in merely two years. This expansion began to seriously concern the regime, which up to this date had considered the film society movement as rather marginal, indeed preferring to ignore it rather than intervene, fearing that this would raise a reaction of support in youth environments. But now the situation seemed to be slipping out of the regime's control, leading the PIDE/DGS to close the Clube de Cinema de Lisboa soon after it had opened, while with Decree-Law 40 572 the authorities sought to impose on the different film societies a statute and federative organization under close government control. This is similar to what would later be established by Decree-Law 40 900 relative to academic associations.

In the meantime, the press launched an intense campaign aimed at the delegitimation of the film society movement and cinema magazines, which were described as subordinate to Moscow and vehicles of communist propaganda. While the effective relations between this movement and the PCP are indeed undeniable, it is also true that the film societies and the aesthetic-political choices of neorealism responded to a thirst for the vanguard and internationalization that was increasingly felt by young Portuguese intellectuals and students. For this group, it was difficult to find in the meanders of the official culture any satisfaction of these new requirements, hence the cultural and aesthetic appeal of neorealism easily also became a political choice. In this perspective, up to at least the early 1960s, the PCP was very probably not only the main adversary of the New State at a political level, but also the main antagonistic force in the cultural sphere. On the other hand, by the end of the 1950s – significantly, concomitantly with the crisis and fragmentation of the communist world – the neorealist hegemony also began to be discussed, with the affirmation of a certain bifurcation of the film society movement. The search for other solutions and other Marxist interpretations which were not submitted to the orthodoxy of the PCP was already recurrent among some young Portuguese students at this time, including in the form of artistic and aesthetic critique that analysed the role of the intellectual and artist in society.

However, more specifically political divisions were exploding in the PCP, which was embarking on its slow loss of consensus among the younger sectors of society. The rigorous materialism of the socialist aesthetic culture was no longer sufficient for the intellectual and social, perhaps more than the political, requirements of the new generations, whose revolt now was not only being directed at economic relations, but also began to involve the super-structural dimension in a progressively more significant manner. While for orthodox Marxists only a change of economic relations would carry forward a change also in the area of human relations, culture and female emancipation, for the young heterodox Marxists the urgent need for change could not wait for the revolution of the production system.

This transformation is evident in the case of Manuel Villaverde Cabral[19] who, in 1957 at the age of seventeen, started to participate in the activities of Cineclube ABC, moving on to *Imagem* in 1958 and writing film reviews for the homonymous magazine, as well as for the film supplement of *Diário de Lisboa*, *Êxito*. This author, for example, portrayed a total absence of topics linked to sexuality in neorealist aesthetics, which to a certain extent corresponded at a political level to the pressure exerted by the PCP for its militants 'to behave with decorum'. Therefore, the appearance and dissemination among young people and especially among students of anti-authoritarian tendencies favoured the rejection of the rigid doctrine of the PCP and an approximation to the organizations of the new left, which were more open in this regard (Henry 2006). In spite of these manifestations of heterodoxies, the role of the film society movements and in particular of *Imagem* as channels of participation and networks of mobilization was fairly important, as is demonstrated by the fact that this was where many student leaders began their militancy. Furthermore, it is also important to emphasize that in the actual plans of the PCP the film societies should train the members of more modest origins, with the objective of penetrating the universities.

The large-scale imprisonment of film society members should be viewed in this perspective, especially from 1963 onwards – that is, immediately after the major academic crisis of 1962. As a consequence of this wave of repression, various leaders of film societies and militants of the PCP, including Manuel Villaverde Cabral himself, left the country to find refuge in Paris, where many participated in the first Maoist split in 1964. The definitive rupture with the party corresponded to the rejection of aesthetic neorealism, considered as 'equivalent to moderation and political pacifism' (Henry 2006: 487). The PCP began to lose control not only of cultural life but also of the political opposition, having been for years the leading figure of a real crusade against hegemony, an alternative to that of the New State. However, this is the story of the following years, while at this time, the end of 1956, the university and youth conflicts were still standing on very different terrain, that of the corporate defence of academic autonomy.

The Plan of the PCP for the Universities

In order to enable a better understanding of the organization of the activism that characterized the student conflicts of the late 1950s and early 1960s, it may be useful, even if this means going rather ahead in time, to examine the PCP's mobilization plan for the student sector. The plan was discovered in the copious amounts of documentation apprehended during the large-scale wave of imprisonment that, following the 1962 crisis, affected workers and students especially of Lisbon and Setúbal, but clearly referred to previous years. On 13 June 1962, a police press release was published in *Diário de Notícias* aimed at clarifying 'aspects of the action of the so-called Portuguese Communist Party',[20] unveiled through a PCP document entitled 'Some experiences of the youth movement in the association of legal and illegal work'. This document recognizes several errors in the action of the MUDJ, extinct in 1957, and in the various attempts aimed at creating a broad-based organization composed of students, young people and workers through structures such as the Movimento Nacional de Estudantes (National Student Movement, MNE) and the União da Juventude Portuguesa (Portuguese Youth Union, UJP). In the document it is admitted that there are no conditions for such structures to operate at a national level, and emphasis is placed on the pressing need for an organization that could associate legal with illegal work:

A correct association of legal work with illegal work means that we should guide all young and progressive communists towards legal activity within mass organizations. We should ensure that all young communists are made fully aware that it is their duty of honour to become involved with young people, to leave narrowly focused groups, seek to be attentive to popular demands and forms of combat that best correspond to the needs and aspirations of each youth sector ... Among the legal organizations at the disposal of young people: student associations, clubs, syndicates, sports and cultural groups in companies, camping, scouts and excursionist groups, film societies, newspapers and legal bulletins, certain sectors of the Mocidade Portuguesa, standing committees.[21]

It is difficult to investigate to what extent this ambitious project of the PCP was accomplished. However, it was certainly a plan that more than rivalled any youth framework initiative programmed by the New State. The PIDE/DGS press release also illustrated how, according to the reconstruction produced by the political police, the plan had been accomplished in previous years, especially through the proliferation of new associations in which PCP members very often achieved positions of leadership, through the constitution of defined unity lists which introduced young people inclined towards collaboration with the party.

The action of these young people was always controlled by the party's members, as would emerge on the pages of the communist news bulletin *O militante*, No. 72, which also incited members of the clandestine party to participate as much as possible in legal organizations. Also according to the PIDE/DGS report, the Portuguese Youth Union was created along these lines, which legally aggregated young people of all professions, including students with or without religious or political tendencies, with the objective of debating their problems and establishing social occasions that, 'through dances, excursions, walks and other forms of fraternization, would convey stronger contact between young people, in favour of the PCP'.[22]

It was also stressed that, because of contrasts between students and workers, the National Student Movement had been formed in 1959. In the words of the PIDE/DGS, this body had expanded its sphere of action, seeking to adapt as far as possible to the present conditions in the universities, to become a movement that would have gathered the majority of the 'academic mass', 'not suspecting that some students acting within it were members of the party'.[23] Furthermore, the press release indicated that, while all these organizations had an ephemeral life, the PCP continued its constant action in the academic associations. This aspect of the strategy was inferred through documents found during the capture of the student José Manuel Bernardino, a PCP militant and the member responsible for the student sector with the pseudonym of 'Rogério', and former secretary general of RIA (Sabino et al. 2009: 49), who was imprisoned by the PIDE/DGS at the end of May 1962 (ibid.: 52).

As an example of this conduct, the political police press release described the political action of Bernardino himself, who, as a young activist of the PCP, had acted as a 'more aware and combative student in the so-called legal conflicts' during the period 1956–1957 as a leader of the Lisbon University Film Society, at this time also having become a member of the board of the Associação de Estudantes do IST (Student Association of the IST, AEIST) and in 1957 a member of a 'civic electoral committee of the university students of Lisbon' with the objective of supporting the opposition candidate, General Humberto Delgado, in the presidential elections. Lastly, having been born in Angola, he became a member of the board of the House of the Students of the Empire in the academic year 1958/59. As is evident, these were all legal organizations in which he had been elected, according to the PIDE/DGS, without anyone knowing of his membership of the PCP.

The verisimilitude of the reconstruction produced by the PIDE/DGS is confirmed, apart from the fact that the described plan is coherent with the PCP's traditional strategy of entryism which was also adopted in relation to the Colonial War, by an identical plan, but restricted to the student sector, presented through a pamphlet of the Movimento Democrático Estudantil (Student Democratic Movement, MDE) dated 1972.[24] This document of a later date, once again highlighted the need for two spheres, legal and illegal. The legal sphere was to be directed at mobilizing the rather non-politicized student mass through the maximum use of all licit possibilities of participation. In turn, the illegal sphere was to be formed by a core of highly politicized people with strong doctrinal education following the orthodox principles of the PCP, for the purpose of indentifying, on a case-by-case basis, the most appropriate objectives and strategies for the contingent situation.

These considerations will be important to understand the great wave of unrest which was concentrated in 1962 (analysed in the next chapter), the peak of circumstances opened in 1958 by the candidature of General Delgado to the presidential elections. The crisis of 1962 emerges not as a spontaneous or improvised event, but rather as the outcome of a highly attentive and intense mobilization effort conducted by the PCP over a number of years.

Notes

1. Álvaro Cunhal insisted on similar positions in *O Radicalismo Pequeno-Burguês de Fachada Socialista*, published underground for the first time in 1970.

2. In respect to the interpretation of Salazarism as a 'border fascism', see Adinolfi (2007).

3. Paolo Ungari, an Italian law historian, has shown that one aspect that distinguishes the essence of the encoding of the law under authoritarian regimes, in the specific case of those fascist-based, is the attempt to resolve social conflicts and divisions through legislative means – i.e. by considering the law as a structural source of society (cf. Ungari 1963: 67). For the author, this means viewing the legal technique as 'hardly technical but very ideological' and, ultimately, transforming it into an instrument of violence. These considerations could also be useful to analyse how the Portuguese New State approached the control of social conflict and political opposition (ibid.).

4. In spite of being a dictatorship, the New State established, in the Constitution, the holding of legislative presidential elections and elections for parish councils, since only popular vote could provide the internal and external legitimacy that it needed. However, the electoral results were always controlled so as to guarantee the victory of the National Union's candidate or list, and all the elections were fraudulent. The presidential elections of 1949 and 1958 were two critical moments for the regime, in that major popular mobilizations upheld the candidates of the opposition, Norton de Matos and Humberto Delgado. Considering that, constitutionally, the President of the Republic had the power to dismiss the President of the Council, one can easily understand the relevance of these elections. Although the control, electoral fraud and repression managed, in the two cases, to ensure that the regime's candidate would win, in order to prevent further risks, Salazar abolished the direct election of the Head of State in 1958.

5. For a deeper analysis of this police force, see Flunser Pimentel (2007a).

6. On the influence of Italian secret police on the Portuguese one, see Flunser Pimentel (2007a), Canali (2004) and Ivani (2009). The significance of this sigla has never been clearly explained. The most accredited meanings are as follows: Opera Volontaria per la Repressione dell'Antifascismo (Voluntary Work for the Repression of Antifascism), Organizzazione di Vigilanza e Repressione dell'Antifascismo (Organization of Surveillance and Repression of Antifascism) and Organo di Vigilanza dei Reati Antistatali (Surveillance Body of Crimes Against the State).

7. For a deeper analysis of this issue, see Rosas (2009).

8. Decree-Law 26 643, article 117. In 1947, Decree-Law 36 387 extended the security measures, already in force for common criminals, to cover political crimes. This stated that people who were convicted of crimes against state security and who had received maximum sentences, or were repeat offenders, or were accused of terrorism were subject to the 'law applicable to hardened criminals' (i.e. the indefinite extension of their sentence for successive periods). See Teles Pereira (1999: 442) and Accornero (2014).

9. Decree-Law 27 058 of 30 September 1936. Although the inspiration of this militia was the Italian 'Milizia Volontaria per la Sicurezza Nazionale' (Voluntary Militia

for National Security, MVSN), the sadly famous Blackshirts (*Camice Nere*), and in part the Sturmabteilung (Assault Divisions, SA), the Portuguese Legion was not a partisan militia like the MVSN or SA, but a body of the State, directly under the Ministry of the Interior and, in the case of crisis, that of war. This difference was also justified by the reason that in Portugal, in contrast to Italy and Germany, the militia was not an instrument of affirmation of the regime, having only been created afterwards. See Rodrigues 1996.

10. Estatuto da Associação Académica de Coimbra, 1961. The statutes of the student associations of Lisbon and Porto established the same rules.
11. Ibid.
12. 'Students of the Higher Technical Institute protest against the occupation of their school by fosterers of the war of the Atlantic Pact', in Avante!, VI, number 217, February 1952. The fact that the PCP information body stresses the heterogeneity of the forces that participated in the contestation is coherent with the strategy of unity in the anti-fascist fight that had guided its party's politics since the end of the Second World War and was underlying the creation of the Movimento de Unidade Democrática (MUD) and its youth wing MUDJ (MUD Juvenil).
13. MUDJ document, 24 June 1947, seized by the PIDE/DGS, in IAN/TT-PIDE/DGS-SC-50/46-2513, folio 8.
14. Ibid.
15. Ibid.
16. Ibid.
17. Ibid.
18. Cit. by Braga da Cruz (2001).
19. Manuel Villaverde Cabral is an important Portuguese sociologist. A member of the PCP and engaged in various intellectual activities – mainly linked to the cinema and the arts – he left Portugal in 1962 in the wave of the harsh repression against youth and students that followed the Academic Crisis of 1962 (see below). Exiled in Paris, there he took part, with other Portuguese communist militants, in the first Maoist split in 1963, which led to the creation of the CMLP. Thereafter, he mainly approached the Italian workerism and entered into contact with Italian militants, such as Toni Negri, and founded, with other exiled Portuguese, the political journal Cadernos de Circunstância (Circumstance's Notebooks). Still in Paris, he concluded a doctorate in history on the origins of capitalism in Portugal, a work considered a milestone in the development of social history in Portugal. He also produced the first Portuguese translation, in 1976, of Operai e Capitali (Workers and Capital) by Mario Tronti, a seminal book for workerism.
20. Cf. *Diário de Notícias*, 13 June 1962, pp. 1 and 9.
21. Ibid.
22. Ibid.
23. Ibid.
24. Pamphlet of the Student Democratic Movement, December 1972, in IAN/TT-PIDE/DGS-SC-SR-3529/62-3370-Pt.167, folio 160.

Chapter 2

The First Protest Cycle: 1956–1965

The Weakening of the Salazarist System

The Government's Attack on the Autonomy of the Student Associations

In view of the considerations developed in the preceding pages regarding the existence of growing student unrest, the promulgation of Decree-Law 40 900 in Portugal, injurious to academic autonomy, no longer appears as an extemporary decision within pacified relations between the State and students – as the propaganda would wish to show – but rather as a reaction of the regime to the progressive loss of control in the university environment, which had taken place over the entire decade of the 1950s. It was, therefore, in this context that Decree-Law 40 900 emerged. Published on 12 December 1956, it was used to create a standing committee for Inter-school and Social Works of Higher Education establishments, intended to replace the academic associations in the majority of these establishments.

The general meeting which, as noted above, was the highest deliberative body of the academic associations and open to all students, would thus have been closed to the general body of students and open merely to a few delegates of each academic year, excluding the first. Moreover, it was established that the associations could only coordinate activities in special cases and only after specific authorization from the Ministério da Educação Nacional (Ministry of National Education, MEN), which was also necessary to establish international relations. The boards of the associations were henceforth appointed with ministerial authorization and would always have to be controlled by a delegate of the Director of the Faculty, also entrusted with watching over and assuring respect for the established social order.

When the decree was approved on 12 December, students of the most diverse Lisbon universities held a meeting, with the presence of personnel of the Associação Académica de Coimbra (Academic Association of Coimbra, AAC). However, in spite of the continuous mobilizations, appeals and petitions, the government scheduled the ratification of the decree by the National Assembly for 16 January 1957. On that same day, an authorized demonstration gathered in front of the assembly that was described by Marcelo Caetano as orderly and peaceful. Notwithstanding this, groups of students close to the building were attacked by the police. Although there were some precedents in the history of the New State, especially in the 1930s and 1940s, this was a particularly delicate situation because, while it is true that police repression was no novelty, the target of the security forces had primarily been the working class and rural communities. It was quite different to publicly attack the children of the elites, although during the years to follow episodes of this type, but increasingly more violent, were destined to be repeated. However, the competence for the approval of the decree was entrusted, exceptionally, to the Corporate Chamber. In fact, transformed into a non-government bill, the decree was never taken to parliamentary discussion, where this situation caused a legislative void on matters of student associativism; on the one hand, this favoured the arbitrariness of the State's repressive intervention, although, on the other hand, it also boosted the development and politicization of the academic organizations.

1956 and Beyond

The second half of the 1950s represented a decisive period which opened up the possibilities of such a conflictual decade as was the 1960s, in Portugal and in the world. The two-year period 1955–1956 was in fact characterized by a series of events that, while not all were directly interconnected, generally refer to the same search for emancipation and equal rights of a civil society. Some of these events have been recalled above, such as the emergence of one of the largest contemporary movements, the civil rights movement in the United States, and its role in the process of extending the rights affirmed by democracy.

From the other side of the barricade of the Cold War, there was also an event that led to the placing in question, albeit with all the limits of the case, of Stalinist authoritarianism and, ultimately, the stifling of civil society in the communist countries. This episode triggered unexpected effects both in institutional politics and in conflictual activity in the most diverse countries of the world. One of the first consequences was the revolt in Hungary in 1956 which, suffocated by the Soviet authorities in spite of the denouncements made against the excesses of Stalin, contributed to questioning of authoritarianism, but with an even further reaching impact. Other effects of these shocks would become more evident with the passing of time – for example, in the Sino-Soviet conflict and in the proliferation of Maoism.

Apart from causing a turnaround in the political strategy of the actual PCP, these elements led the universe of conflictual action with Marxist undertones, up to then generally monopolized by the communists, to start to fragment into a constellation of more radical organizations. These points will be discussed in more detail below. However, it is necessary at this point to emphasize that it was above all heresies of Marxism that attracted the interest of the student movements as of the second half of the 1960s, in a process of convergence founded on a common anti-authoritarian quest that, in addition to the institutions of bourgeois capitalism – without major distinction between those democratic and those authoritarian – also criticized the communist party structures, considered, on the one hand, too moderate from a political point of view, and on the other hand, too backward with respect to social matters such as, for example, the issue of women's rights.

Thus, all the conditions were created for a restricted movement of national scope, such as the student objection to Decree-Law 40 900, to acquire a resonance and continuity that might perhaps go beyond its actual intentions. However, in 1956, a year generally recalled as that of the debut of the Portuguese student movement – which, while it had already been mobilized on specific occasions, was only now able to be organized in a joint movement of all the universities – the official press gave little importance to the event. While it is true that the unrest was not particularly widespread, also taking into account the small size of the academic world, a keen observer would have seen in it the seeds of an explosion of issues and an action repertoire that would characterize student conflicts over the following decades. Also underestimated was the fact that, through this mobilization, the Portuguese student associations had lived for five years in a legislative void which fostered their development and independence.

Nevertheless, in 1956, the revolt against Decree-Law 40 900 was not the only mobilization that involved students. In fact, merely a month before, in November, the university environment had been imbued with large demonstrations against the Soviet repression of the Hungarian revolution, supported in this case by the actual government, especially through Marcelo Caetano. The newspaper *Diário de Notícias* gave ample coverage, over a month, of the actions of 'solidarity of the Portuguese with the oppressed Hungarian people' and of demonstrations organized by various student sectors, based on ideas of emancipation and freedom paradoxically celebrated by Marcelo Caetano on 7 November in a speech in which he defended 'civil rights and public freedoms'.[1] These manifestations served to activate networks that would soon be used against the actual government.

As some CADC members upheld, the experience of participation in the demonstrations against the USSR thus enabled the successive adherence to the mobilization against Decree-Law 40 900: 'the demand for freedom has reflected internally, boosting domestic interest in political freedom, university autonomy and student associativism'.[2] Thus, while in his speech Caetano emphasized that Russia's attitude had been one of the most violent in the political history of all times and that the events should serve as a lesson to the Portuguese youth for the future of Portugal, in fact this youth was ready to place in practice the lesson learnt, but in the opposite sense desired by the future head of government. On the other hand, the broad mobilization that the government managed to raise around the Hungarian crisis led to the emergence of a counter-mobilization, primarily accomplished by the PCP and directed at unveiling the mystification represented by the fact that 'those who in their own country impose a regime lacking in freedom, organize demonstrations supporting the fight of the Hungarian people' (Pacheco Pereira 2005: 393).

The Shaking Up of the Political Opportunity Structure

Albeit on a small scale, the student unrest of 1956 announced a protest cycle that prepared to spread throughout and transform the country and its regime. Various authors emphasize that, after the wave of internal and external confrontation of the institutional policies that characterized the years between 1958 and 1962, the New State managed to survive, but would never be the same again:

> The regime would manage to survive it, but would never fully recover: nothing would ever be the same again. In contrast to 1947, this did not involve a restoration of strength, of a new lease of life. The recomposition of the regime, required by the reformists and supported by the opposition, involved changes unacceptable to the Salazarists, since they represented, in the long term, the actual overturning, if not the negation, of some essential paradigms held to be unquestionable. On this issue, the elections of 1958 truly marked the beginning of the end of Salazarism and the actual regime. (Rosas 1997: 468–69)

Various factors contributed to weaken the rigid structure of the regime and open the way to trigger the protest cycle, since the period between 1958 and 1962 was one of the most critical times of the regime, characterized by shocks and tensions that violently affected the sphere of institutional politics. In 1958, General Humberto Delgado submitted his candidature for the presidential elections, standing against the regime's candidate Américo Tomás, with the promise of expediting an opening of the political system and dismissing Salazar (which was, indeed an entitlement of the President of the Republic). Supported by all the opposition forces, he achieved major popular consensus which was reflected in large-scale social mobilization, although it was evidently unlikely that he would win the elections. This moment represented merely the onset of critical circumstances in which the fate of the regime appeared to be truly under discussion and, together with other elements at an institutional political and conflictual level, contributed to triggering a real protest cycle. Thousands of supporters, challenging the violent police repression, all followed the electoral campaign in the main cities of the country. Many militants of the opposition to the New State of the 1960s and 1970s identified the Delgado campaign as a sort of political baptism (Accornero and Villaverde Cabral 2011; Accornero 2013b; Accornero 2013c and Accornero 2014). This event was, in fact, the beginnings of mobilization for a large number of the militants who would oppose the New State in the 1960s and 1970s. Various militant students, communists, and those affiliated to the emerging new left organizations, began their political activity at this point.

During the campaign, a petition was organized by high school students of Lisbon in support of the candidature of General Delgado, an initiative that served to gather together some of those who were to create the High School Education of Lisbon Pro-Association Commission in 1960, later the Secondary Education Pro-Association Commission. The foundation of the commission, which orbited around the PCP and was to play an important role in the student unrest of the following years, included the names of many who would become the most active militants during the following twenty years, such as José Luís Saldanha Sanches, Rui d'Espiney, Teresa Tito Morais, Fernando Rosas and his brother Filipe Rosas. Some of them, stepping away from the PCP, would also be found among the leaders of new organizations to the far left, especially Maoist, as of the second half of the 1960s. In fact, the 'Delgado hurricane' not only shook the regime's structures, but also the actual PCP, which was not prepared for this great mobilization which slipped through its control, having attempted 'up to the extent of the absurd to counter its action [being] later utterly dragged along by the *hurricane*' (Pacheco Pereira 2005: 573). Cunhal himself, at the time still in Peniche, would admit, in 1961, that the party had not managed to harvest the opportunities of a pre-insurrection situation, in which it had been superseded by the initiative of the popular masses. However, as indicated by José Pacheco Pereira, it was not only the PCP that was shaken, since: 'The events of 1957 and 1958 presented a cruel portrayal of the Portuguese opposition, divided into small competitive groups, which in turn were even more divided by the vanity of the personalities composing them. Delgado showed the historical depletion of a certain type of opposition, and opened Portuguese politics to the 1960s, when everything was different, harsher, more violent, less accommodating' (ibid.).

A crisis of such a large scale and depth could not fail to be linked to the social changes that Portugal experienced after the Second World War and to international dynamics. After this period, with the electoral defeat of Delgado and the announced victory of the Salazarist candidate Américo Tomás, in fact the strife continued under various forms. One of the outstanding moments of these mobilizations, before the peak of 1962, was the elections of November 1961, the first to take place after the Colonial War.

One of the first consequences of these events at an institutional level was the narrowing of the opportunities of participation of citizens, already by this time very reduced, and, in order to prevent the risk of repetition of such mobilization, the constitutional text was amended, through Law 2100 of August 1959. In this way, the President of the Republic, up to then elected by the citizens, albeit with restricted suffrage, was henceforth elected by a college of 602 members, selected among members of parliament, members of the Corporate Chamber, representatives of the administrative structures of the overseas territories and representatives of the city halls. However, this measure was ineffective, both against the mobilization that had been triggered and that was being channelled into a true protest cycle, and against the other threats that were arriving from inside and outside the regime.

Of these adverse circumstances for the New State, the colonial issue, which ecloded virulently in the early 1960s and to which the regime reacted with the decision of going to war in 1961, certainly represented the most determinant aspect. This was, in particular, because the government's choice of war was not consensual inside the regime, thus causing fragmentation in the highest ranks of the State and leading to a situation of division of the elites potentially favourable to the opening of political opportunities and, indeed, an intensification of mobilization. Therefore, even if it failed, the attempted coup d'état by the Chief of the Defence Staff, Júlio Botelho Moniz, in April 1961 is emblematic. These were the factors that contributed to make the crisis of 1962 the peak of the protest cycle, and which saw an exceptional mobilization of students and workers, during one of the moments of most intense conflict and most dangerous times to the regime's stability. Nevertheless, it already started to peter out in 1963.

The Colonial War

On 22 January 1961, Captain Galvão, already a leader of an attempted coup in 1952, headed a group of twenty-three men, which included eleven militants of the Directorio Revolucionario Ibérico de Liberación (Iberian Revolutionary Directorate for Liberation, DRIL), in an attack that led to the occupation, in the Caribbean Sea, of the passenger liner Santa Maria. This was 'Operation Dulcinea', which aimed to pursue the utopian objective of reaching northern Angola and installing a provisional government there. However, due to the necessity of caring for various wounded people, the ship was forced to dock at the island of Santa Lucia, where the experiment ended.

As shown by Fernando Rosas, when the failed attack by Angolan nationalists on prisons to release the political prisoners took place on 4 February 1961, many journalists were still in Luanda hoping to report the eventual arrival of the passenger liner Santa Maria (Rosas 1997: 248). This fact gives an idea of the critical circumstances that Portugal was experiencing and the international resonance that, in spite of the motto 'proudly alone', the events linked to the Salazarist policy were beginning to receive. Always concerned with the international sphere, the Kennedy administration showed a change of heart with respect to the principle of self-determination of peoples and independence of the colonies, indeed stating that he could no longer continue to support Portugal in the United Nations if the country did not change its policy. Following this new direction, the American services began to support the União dos Povos de Angola (Union of Peoples of Angola, UPA), led by Holden Roberto, which triggered the attacks in northern Angola and which marked the onset of the Colonial War.

This position of the United States contributed to the division of the political elites and especially military staff on the solution to be given to the colonial problem. This division was at the base of the thwarted attempt, in April 1961, of the coup d'état of the Minister of Defence, Botelho Moniz, who, opposed to the military enterprise, had already tried to convince Salazar to desist. On the other hand, these episodes merely added visibility to the pre-existing fractures in Portuguese society, which these critical circumstances brought out and boosted. Thus, 'Botelho Moniz emerged as the military arm of the civil reformist current, as had been outlined since the mid-1950s', and the 'defeat of the April coup, in reality, would be the decisive factor for the survival of Salazarism in the wake of the Delgado affair' (Rosas 1997: 250).

However, the last and most radical attack from the armed forces was the storming of Beja Headquarters, carried out by officials of the middle staff on 1 January 1962, who found support in the most diverse sectors of society. The military plan, which was never actually implemented, consisted of the occupation of the Infantry and headquarters of the GNR of Beja, from which military and civilian formations would emerge with the objective of raising a popular uprising of the entire region. General Delgado had clandestinely entered Portugal with the purpose of leading the revolt, and fled again after the failure of the plan. As stated by Fernando Rosas, Beja represented the swan song, at this stage, of the revolutionary behaviour of the middle staff (Rosas 1997).

In the meantime, while the military elites finally appeared to be united and faithful to Salazar and to the bellicose enterprise, the war and moreover the military conscription process would represent, as will be analysed below, the principal element of dissidence not only in the ranks of the opposition, including student opposition, but also among the actual armed forces, creating the premises for the formation of the movement that led to the revolution of 1974. Therefore, although it is correct that the defence of the empire represented the defence of its very survival to the New State (Costa Pinto 2001), paradoxically the regime could not survive a war of that scale in the long term. Among the opposition, the attitude in relation to the Colonial War, although generally contrary to this enterprise, also portrayed a variety of facets among the different groups, especially with respect to the strategy to be adopted. The PCP had for the first time assumed a declaredly favourable position to the independence of the colonies at the V Congress in 1957. Up to then, the party had maintained an ambiguous position. As suggested by Pacheco Pereira, this was not an anomaly of the Portuguese Communist Party, but rather an attitude that it shared with the communist parties of other colonialist countries, and which was based on the Stalinist idea of distinguishing between different levels of action 'according to the stage of the revolution and the alignment and existence of social classes such as the proletariat' (Pacheco Pereira 2005: 502).

The affirmation of Maoism among Portuguese students as of the late 1960s was therefore a base for a position of more open opposition to the Colonial War. On the other hand, another important difference was emerging between the PCP and the new left-wing groups, in this case relative to the strategy to be adopted in relation to government policies of military conscription. The groups of the radical left, especially the Maoist, which emerged in Portugal during the final stages of the regime, were more openly supportive than the PCP of both desertion and resistance, through flight and exile, as opposed to military conscription. In turn, while at the beginning of the conflict the PCP had also encouraged desertion, it later began to ask its militants to enter the army and, once incorporated, to carry out propaganda and politicization work. This strategy was not unknown and was indeed a source of concern to the authorities and above all to the armed forces. In a report dated 1970, the then Deputy Chief of the Army Staff, General António Augusto dos Santos, thus denounced:

> Immediately after the onset of the subversion in Angola, in 1961, the PCP, the most important revolutionary organization, disseminated specific guidelines inviting soldiers to desert ... Subsequently, the PCP reviewed this initial attitude, henceforth advocating only desertion en mass, as a form of weakening the armed forces and as a process of discrediting the fight for the overseas [territories]. The PCP started to order its militants and sympathizers to enlist and, once in the armed forces, to begin to foster actions of contestation

and revolt, based on situations of discontent of military personnel, created by injustices and excesses.[3]

I shall return at various points to discuss these issues, especially since, as of the late 1960s, the opposition to the Colonial War became the main factor of mobilization of all the forces that fought against the regime, being the principal common denominator between the most varied political areas.

The Academic Crisis of 1962

Political Process and Mobilization

After the events of 1956, the celebration of Dia do Estudante (Student's Day) became a particularly important event in the activities of the academic associations. The celebrations programme, in addition to recreational aspects, also began to feature the debate of social issues linked to university life and, gradually, real political problems. By 1957, Student's Day was celebrated in Lisbon and included, as well as participation of the Círculo de Iniciação Teatral Académica de Coimbra (Theatrical Initiation and Academic Circle of Coimbra, CITAC) and a concert by the Musical Youth in collaboration with the Symphonic Orchestra, a conference on 'Life in the University Campus'.

In 1961, the Student's Day was once again celebrated in Lisbon from 16 to 19 March, with a programme that covered discussions on the problems of university residences, transport and health. Also in this direction was the clear interest in insisting, in contrast to what had been done up to then, on the connection between the various academic centres of the country, of which the holding of Jornada do Estudante (Student's Day) in November 1960 and I University Social Meeting of February 1961 were a direct consequence. It should also be noted in particular that, in 1961, the publication of the Academic Association of Coimbra, *Via Latina*, presented poetry of authors of the opposition such as Manuel Alegre. These initiatives contributed to creating the roots for the major unrest that broke out in Lisbon in 1962, the first real mass movement at the Portuguese university.

The pretext for the outburst of the crisis was the prohibition of the Student's Day which should have been held in Lisbon on 24 March. The programme of this event involved topics that were not particularly different from previous years, including a colloquium on 'The integration of the student in the university', a sports festival and a social dinner in the new canteen of the university campus. A fortnight previously, the authorities had already prohibited the holding of the 1st National Meeting of Students, which, in the meantime, also took place in Coimbra, with the discussion of the problem of access to university. In this case involving a delicate topic, especially considering the three principles approved in the final communiqué: '1st, urgent democratization of education, through effective measures; 2nd, suppression of unjust economic discrimination, which degenerates national intelligence; 3rd, extension of university education to all Portuguese students, regardless of considerations of political, racial order or any other type' (Medeiros Ferreira 1998: 188).

These were no longer addressed demands of a corporate nature, that is, aimed at defending the interests and autonomy of those within the institution, as indeed had occurred in 1956, but started to show a demand for an opening in favour of those who, due to the rigidity of the structure, were still excluded. Moreover, note should be made of the emergence of the concept of 'democratization' in the student repertoire of contention, a concept that, while still subject to changes according to the times and environments in which it was used, would be the cornerstone of student activity in the following years. It is also interesting to observe that this student debate reflected a parallel debate that had swept through their institutions a few years earlier. The social changes that had emerged since the second half of the 1950s had, in fact, exerted strong pressure on the guidelines of the regime's education policy, and it is in this perspective that some of the school reforms adopted by the Minister of National Education, Francisco Leite Pinto (1955–1961), should be interpreted. Generally recalled as having been responsible for the contestation of 1956, Leite Pinto was also the minister who carried out some of the most significant education reforms, in accordance with the industrialist positions that had become firmly implanted in the New State during the 1950s.

As any political regime, even if authoritarian, the New State could not be completely insensitive to the major socio-cultural changes that were taking place in the country, particularly since they were induced by two parallel and complementary movements, the processes of industrialization and urbanization. It was in these dynamics that the education reforms introduced by Leite Pinto were placed, as was the ordering of a 'Quantitative Analysis of the Portuguese School Structure (1950–1959)' from the Economic Statistics Research Centre, which was one of the first sociological studies conducted in Portugal.[4] The direct stimulus to the accomplishment of this analysis not only came from the commitments assumed by Portugal under the Mediterranean Regional Project, but also from the awareness, among the more advanced sector of the regime, of the need to adjust the education system to the new requirements brought in by the process of industrialization. Hence, it was not only the necessity to train more qualified workers that imposed an adjustment of the school system, but also the urgency in responding to the new aspirations derived from contemporary society. This does not mean that there existed, in this drive to modernization, any desire for social justice, but rather that, for the New State, as for the majority of political regimes, authoritarian or not, it was in fact impossible to completely ignore social change, thus requiring concessions to some demands.

In this sense, the reform represented a conflict prevention response to a certain extent and it is only in this perspective that it is possible to understand reforms that appear contrary to the elitist orientation at the base of the ideology of the New State. Among these reforms, the introduction of the single school was especially important due to the increased compulsory education of four years, which was introduced in 1956 for boys and extended to girls in 1960, and later the creation of a committee to study the unification of the 'Preparatory Cycle of Technical Education and the 1st Cycle of High School Education'. This project would have enabled postponing the student's choice between high school and a vocational training institution, since it was considered that it was too early to make this choice at the end of primary school. Furthermore, the unification would serve to expand compulsory education to six years.

This limited democratization of education was clearly not derived from an ideological choice, but from the need for economic development and therefore, in Portugal as in other countries governed by different regimes, it was only in the context of a reasonable industrial development that the principles of the single school began to constitute an acceptable standard to regulate the transformation of the national education system.[5] Various reforms were also adopted with respect to the university world, again directed towards equalizing the different sources of education. In addition, a 'New Plans of the Engineering Courses Taught at Portuguese Universities' was promulgated through Decree 40 378 in 1955, which allowed the IST and the Faculdade de Engenharia da Universidade do Porto (Faculty of Engineering of Porto University, FEUP) to confer a doctoral degree in some specialities. In 1957 it was the turn of the Fine Arts course to be reformed, so as to be practically equivalent to a university course, and in the same year, the course programme of the Faculty of Letters was reformed, extending the course to five years and adding various subjects.

This requirement to open up the university structures shows coherence between the issues that had been debated at government level a little earlier and the main topics of the student movement at this stage. This represents a typical condition of protest cycles, as Sidney Tarrow emphasizes with respect to the Italian protest cycle which also involved, in its student aspect, an open debate among the elites on university reform:

> The demands and actions of the students did not emerge from nothing; they were the effect of a longer-lasting and widespread movement that had arisen in the midst of the two main political subcultures of the country in the early 1960s and that had developed their internal conflicts and political interests ... The problem of the school reform

fuelled one of the most difficult controversies of the political history of post-war Italy, but not primarily because of the student movement. In fact it divided parties, associations, teachers, assistant staff, and parents. (Tarrow 1989: 133–34)

And moreover:

People go out into the streets and protest in response to deeply felt grievances and opportunities. But this produces a protest cycle only when structural cleavages are both profound and visible, and when opportunities for mass protest are opened up by the political system. Cycles begin within institutions through organized forms of collective action. (ibid.: 13)

In the case of the student unrest in Portugal, there is a similar trend: the issues debated in the institutions crossed the boundary line of the government sphere to extend to the sphere that researchers of collective action refer to as 'challengers'.[6] However, the major difference in relation to the Italian case, and which concerns the authoritarian nature of the Portuguese regime, is that the actual debate relative to the modernization discussed among the elites of the country was about to be eliminated by Salazar, who, after the repeated threats to the New State, imposed an imperative return to the rural and traditional principles expressed in what was known as the 'Braga values'. These would be the essential principles of Salazarism as Salazar himself stated in his speech on the occasion of the '10th Year of the National Revolution', proclaimed in Braga in 1936. These values, in addition to the most known – God, Fatherland, Authority, Family and Work – and indeed underlying these, there were also the principles of anti-communism, anti-parliamentarianism and the primacy of a rural lifestyle over the destabilizing and corrupting changes of industrial development. It should be stressed that none of these values escaped the increasingly more radical criticism and questioning of the student contestation. Fernando Rosas suggests that this effort made by Salazar to defend the unquestionable values of the regime, not only in view of the threats of the opposition but also of the reformists and industrialists within the actual government, had been unfolding since the 1950s (Rosas 1997: 459–60).

While these episodes indicate the burgeoning intensification of the mobilization and political radicalization that led to the revolution of April 1974, in the shorter term, the years following the major crisis of 1962 represented a period when the regime, in order to survive, was forced to compact its ranks, weed out disloyal people, heighten repression and strongly reaffirm its actual original ideals against the industrialist and modernizing deviation of the previous decade. And, above all, it intransigently continued to pursue the bellicose enterprise that had only just begun. In brief, the regime drastically and rapidly closed the fissure that had opened up in its solidity.

The Peak of the Protest

24 March 1962, the date scheduled for the celebration of Student's Day and as a consequence of its prohibition, was the beginning of a prolonged academic crisis that lasted until June, met up with a simultaneous major unrest among the workers, especially following 1 May 1962. The prohibition of the academic celebration was accomplished through the deployment of numerous public security police agents inside the university campus. On 26 March, the RIA responded by declaring formal academic mourning at a general meeting attended by close to two thousand students. On the following day, the recently installed Minister of National Education, Lopes de Almeida, received a delegation of associative leaders who convinced him to withdraw the veto, and hence the celebration of Student's Day was planned for 7 and 8 April, with the same programme that had previously been established. However, on 5 April the government once again prohibited the celebration, with the justification that it had not received its programme.

In the meantime, the academic associations gathered all their forces in order to organize widespread mobilization, which would imply the mass involvement of the students of the three university cities of Lisbon, Porto and Coimbra. In addition to stimulating this uprising, first the veto and then the presence of the police inside in the university area caused a crisis within the regime, with the resignation of Marcelo Caetano from the position of Rector of Lisbon University, which he had held since 1959, and the resignation of Coronel Homero de Matos from the Directorate-General for the PIDE/DGS. Lastly, by the end of the year, the actual Minister of National Education, Lopes de Almeida, who had held the position for only a year, was replaced by Inocêncio Galvão Teles.

From 9 to 11 May, around eight hundred students installed themselves in the canteen of Lisbon University campus in support of twenty-one of their colleagues who were there conducting a hunger strike. On 10 May, Lisbon University Senate held an exceptional meeting at which, after hearing from José Medeiros Ferreira, the delegate of the students of the Faculty of Letters, they resolved to grant the students a further hour to evacuate the occupied premises. The deadline, which expired at 19.45, was not respected, and the students were evacuated from the university canteen at around 4 the next morning by the public security police, being detained by direct order of the Ministry of the Interior. The evacuation operation was overblown: the eight hundred or so students, who included eighty-four girls, were forced into police trucks and were all placed at the disposal of the police for interrogation, with many being released that same afternoon, while others were kept behind for subsequent investigation.

On 18 May, the minister of national education declared that any attempt to create bodies aimed at the unification of student associations and joint youth political action at university was illegal.[7] After attributing all the blame on the students' stubbornness in view of the 'clear willingness of the authorities', the minister stressed that it had been necessary to suspend the legally constituted management bodies of the academic associations, and to prohibit those that operated outside of the law. It was also stated that the student unrest had been fired up by political agents who had subjugated the easily influenced youth masses, who were 'rather unaware of the foundations of social interaction'. Finally, the government sought to inform public opinion on the intervention of the police, explaining that, although there was no provision preventing the exercise of authority by the security forces in the university zone, it was the government's firm desire that discipline inside education establishments should always be upheld by the academic authorities. Moreover, it stressed that, since the management bodies of the student associations of Lisbon and Coimbra were suspended, any attempts to hold association meetings would be illegal, especially any referred to as plenary, as would the operation of any bodies aimed at a unification of associations for joint action.[8]

Ultimately, on 21 May of the same year, Decree-Law 44 357 was published, which represented the legislative side of the violent repression of the student associations. This legislation established that the Ministry of Education could always order disciplinary proceedings against the students of schools under its tutelage, freely appoint teachers and apply any penalty stipulated in the legislation that regulated this matter. Based on these rules, around fifty students from three academies who had been distinguished in the recent unrest were suspended. On 29 June, through ministerial order, the twenty-one students who had declared a hunger strike from 9 to 11 May were expelled, and than banned from all schools, whilein Coimbra, thirty-four students, among whom were five leaders, were sentenced to being suspended from university for six months and banned for up to two years from all schools.

Innovations and Resources of the Movement of 1962

The year of 1962 thus represented the great debut of the students as protagonists of the conflictual action in Portugal, a debut that extended into a true protest cycle, through which these new players definitively entered into the Portuguese scenario of insurrection, remaining at least until the end of the regime. As stated by Fernando Rosas: 'The importance of the Academic

Crisis of 1962 not only resides in the conquering of the student movement for anti-fascist resistance, but also in the particularly important role that it would play in this struggle as a whole, at least until the early 1970s' (Rosas 2012: 33). The innovation of the protest's repertoire, whether from the point of view of demands or actions, thus entered into the memory of collective action in Portugal, passing from one movement to another, until reaching, as various authors have demonstrated, the movements that characterized the PREC, such as that of the home dwellers (Ramos Pinto 2007: 91–92).

The principal innovation was undoubtedly that of occupation. This new form of action also forced the authorities to redesign the measures of police intervention in student conflicts, through rules that permitted, when requested by the University Senate and after receiving the consent of the Ministry of the Interior, the intervention of the security forces inside education establishments. The new legislation relative to the criminal prosecution of students also represented a response to the conflictual innovations introduced by the student movement. The importance of this innovation was testified by the creation, on the part of the Home Office and the actual police, of a specific file designed to collect all relevant documentation concerning the 'student crisis'. As often occurs, changes in the area of contentious politics also impose changes and innovations in the management of public order.

On the other hand, the resorting to an action such as a hunger strike also appears to have been most innovative, since not many examples of this type of action are found in the history of Portuguese social movements, and even less so in the history of the student movement. However, while occupations were to be highly successful in the future of the student unrest, hunger strikes would only be widely used in prisons, where it was almost always adopted by political prisoners and was one of the primary causes of punishment by the prison authorities.[9]

The End of the Protest Cycle

Repression and Demobilization

As has been noted above, through the imprisonment that occurred during the months following the crisis of 1962, the PIDE/DGS had managed to uncover the network and action developed by the PCP up to this date, aimed at stimulating and mobilizing the academic environment. However, the aspect on which the PIDE/DGS showed great ignorance was the fact that, from 1962 onwards, the panorama of the student dissent had become more complex, with the fragmentation of the currents of opposition to the regime. The purpose of press release of the PIDE/DGS, which disclosed the PCP document entitled 'Some experiences of the youth movement in the association of legal with illegal work',[10] was explicitly to show public opinion the source of the recent episodes that had altered the life of the city of Lisbon throughout the entire month of May. After a long period of continuous threats to the stability of the regime, derived from many directions – democratic opposition, armed forces, colonial, student and worker movements – this press release of the PIDE/DGS, not by chance disclosed through the SNI, was intended to demonstrate that the situation was fully under control.

An obvious attempt was also made to impute the source of this profound and widespread discontent on an exogenous cause, which was attributed to a specific strategy drawn up in Moscow. Likewise, this was also the case of the major mobilization in support of Delgado in 1958 and the emergence of the colonial liberation movements. In fact, the admission of endogenous conflict within the State was unthinkable, since the actual essence of corporatism resides in the idea of the sublimation of conflicts between the different bodies of the nation into a process of social pacification. Indeed, the causes of the academic crisis of 1962 were entirely attributed to the subversive strategy of the PCP 'without any margin of doubt'.[11]

That the student and worker mobilization had been coordinated and in part stimulated through the network and logistic resources of the PCP is a fairly obvious fact, since at this time the Communist Party was still the main organization of the opposition to the regime. However, apart from the presence of other ideological components, such as Catholicism, in this contestation, the authorities underestimated the fact that since the crisis showed mass characteristics, this was because there was profound discontent circulating in practically all sectors of society: universities, church, armed forces and factories.

This amplitude of mobilization is explained by three complementary factors, all of which are necessary: the fact that the regime had been undergoing a period of deep crisis since the elections in 1958; the fact that effective mobilization networks and resources existed and were available (where the majority were indeed the result of the action of the PCP); and finally, the fact of the existence of actors willing to be mobilized. This last point was also related to the major social and economic changes that led to higher expectations and the search for opportunities among different sectors of society.

After 1962 the social conflict greatly diminished in amplitude. At the same time it became more radical, and consequently the countermeasures aimed at a 'return to order' were intensified. The repressive action was not only resolved by contingent measures, but was also strengthened through an exponential increase in the control and investigation of all student activity by the political police. As was noted in the preceding chapter, on 24 May 1962 the PIDE/DGS imprisoned five PCP militants from whom documentation was seized that confirmed, in the opinion of the authorities, the communist influence in the university unrest. This documentation was also used in successive action by the political police aimed at dismantling the PCP's organizational network in the university. Among the five prisoners,[12] the only student was José Manuel Mendonça de Oliveira Bernardino, of the UJP. The prison history of Bernardino was in fact one of the longest and harshest of the students imprisoned at this time, demonstrating the evident interest of the PIDE/DGS in displaying a message of intimidation to other students through an exemplary sentence.

The imprisonment of Bernardino inaugurated a wave of repression of exceptional intensity against the students which extended throughout the entire year of 1962[13] and, after a slight attenuation in 1963, continued in 1964 and 1965 – that is, until the end of the first student protest cycle that I have situated between 1956 and 1965. From December 1964 to January 1965, following almost two years of meticulous investigations carried out by the PIDE/DGS, the repression began with the imprisonment of Bernardino and continued based on the documents seized on that occasion. On 6 December, the pages of the mainstream Portuguese daily newspapers announced the imprisonment of various members of the PCP, which included, it was highlighted, eighteen university students.[14]

A note of the Ministry of the Interior was also published aimed at disclosing the successes of PIDE/DGS investigations to counter the subversive activities of the block generically defined as communist, in particular following an explosive attempt that took place on 5 October. In fact, it was soon discovered that the perpetrators of the attempt, one of the first conflictual actions of this type carried out in Portugal during the enforcement of the New State, were linked to the FAP which, as seen before, was the first Maoist faction to have broken away from the PCP. It is difficult to understand whether the PIDE/DGS already knew of this split or if it considered the FAP to be an armed wing of the PCP. It was described as an organization 'formed above all by university students', of whom eleven were already detained, and by other young people of different professions. On the other hand, other FAP members had evaded imprisonment and fled into exile abroad.

Once again, the authorities insisted that their investigations confirmed firm establishment of the PCP in the academic environment, indeed failing to distinguish between the FAP and PCP. The detention of these young people was ultimately and completely attributed to their activity in subversive organizations and not to their actual student action. Nuno Álvares Pereira was imprisoned on 6 December, being defined as a high-standing member of the PCP and 'former university student who, in addition to fostering unrest, represented one of the communist cells present among university students'.[15]

Nuno Álvares Pereira, who had gone underground, and lived in hiding 'at the expense of the PCP'[16] for close to two years, was located when he met up with another communist militant who had also been imprisoned, António José Crisóstomo Teixeira, a student of the Faculty of Science and also a PCP leader in the student environment. At the time of his capture, Nuno Álvares Pereira used the false identity of João Miguel dos Santos and the false profession of private school teacher. Simultaneously, an announcement was made of the proceedings, in Boa Hora plenary court, of 20-year-old José Luís Saldanha Sanches, future leader of the Maoist organization the Movimento Reorganizativo do Partido do Proletariado (Reorganizational Movement of the Proletariat Party, MRPP), imprisoned at the end of April and, at that time an important personality of the student sector of the PCP, while a student of the Faculty of Law. The prison history of Saldanha Sanches, with four distinct periods of detention, was also chosen to be an example to others (Accornero and Villaverde Cabral 2011; Accornero 2013a, 2013c, 2014),[17] as indeed regularly happened to students – and prisoners in general – who were most structured within opposition organizations.

By the end of 1964, twenty-eight students remained in prison awaiting proceedings, and this number was to grow in the new year. In the meantime, the wave of repression against the university reached its peak on the night of 20/21 January 1965, at the vigil of a commemorative manifestation of the student fight of 1956, with the arrest of around fifty associative leaders, in a manoeuvre that effectively decapitated, at a single stroke, the entirety of the communist student organization of Lisbon. The news was disclosed on 22 January in the mainstream daily national newspapers through a note from the SNI, which underlined the fact that the operation had been the outcome of the 'continued pursuit by the PIDE/DGS to repress the activities against the security of the nation'.[18] Also included among the arrested student leaders of the PCP were Filipe and Fernando Rosas. Fernando Rosas, a law student who had been active since his high school days, was at the time an important militant of the PCP, albeit destined to a political evolution more orientated towards Maoism which would lead him, at the end of the 1960s, to appear among the founding members of the MRPP. As was the case of other figures within structured opposition organizations – up to this time still the PCP, but a little later, as will be seen, also in different groups – he was dealt a harsher sentence than many of his colleagues who, in various cases, only participated in student activities and had no direct contact with any specific political organization.

Although some of the students imprisoned on 21 January 1965 were not communists, such as the Catholic Luís Salgado Matos, the clear objective of the

PIDE/DGS was to destroy the PCP's activity in the universities, which, after a large number of arrests, searches and seized documents, the police knew in detail. For the same purpose, control was intensified on legal student organizations, such as the actual academic associations. The arrests would continue throughout the year, so that, having decapitated the PCP's organizational network in the universities, it could attempt to dismantle the communist structure of the industrial area south of the River Tagus. In general, the processes that involved students, especially those of interest in the context of this study, also became increasingly more summary and extensive, peaking on 11 August 1965 with twenty-seven imputed, where the majority was represented by the nineteen students imprisoned during the great police action of 21 January 1965. Thanks to this repressive wave, the academic milieu lost almost all their leaders, for the most part communists.

The crisis of 1962 was therefore the pinnacle of a particularly critical period for the regime, during which the most diverse social sectors – from the most habitual, such as the workers, to the newest, such as the Catholics and middle staff of the army – showed their displeasure with Salazar. The survival of the dictatorship after these circumstances was not entirely secure. The end of this crisis was accompanied by a partial restructuring of the political system, with the elimination of the direct election of the President of the Republic, by a recrudescence of the repression against the political opposition and by the beginning of the Colonial War.

The imprisonment of the senior echelons of the PCP was part of this process aimed at 'reconsolidating' the regime, but it also had a series of unexpected consequences, above all in the academic milieu which, while on the one hand became quieter for a few years due to the imprisonments, expulsions and exiles, but on the other hand started to become more radical. These incarcerations and those that followed, albeit it in a less intensive form, throughout 1965, were very important from the point of view of the process of political radicalization. Many of the communist student leaders imprisoned during this wave would transfer to the radical left, some of whom would become founders of the most important Portuguese Maoist organizations – such as the MRPP – which agitated and sharpened the political conflict in the final years of the regime, and even during the revolutionary process, between 1974 and 1975. These developments occurred for different reasons. The repression against the PCP contributed, on the one hand, to the dismantling of the organization of this party, leaving an empty space that was rapidly occupied by other formations of the radical left that had emerged in the meantime. On the other hand, the strong repression of 1964–1965 had the effect of disaccrediting the PCP, particularly among the younger activists, who began to strongly criticize the party for its moderate and legalist strategy, as well as for its attitude, considered ambiguous, towards the

Colonial War. The status of violence as a means of political struggle started to shift drastically during this phase, to become hegemonic with the radical left during the 1970s, although rarely was this embodied in real actions of armed combat. The PCP considered that active violence should not be transformed into a form of combat, because its success could lead to greater repression by the State, and the use of more aggressive means should be limited to a form of defence and resistance. In contrast, for the organizations of the extreme left that were emerging at this time, violence represented an essential means of political struggle: the violence of the state legitimated revolutionary violence, making it necessary. Moreover, as noted above, during these years the founders and principal militants of the FAP, the first Portuguese Maoist organization that had theorized the need for revolutionary violence, were imprisoned following the first actions of armed struggle. The students imprisoned in 1964–1965 were given the opportunity to meet these militants face-to-face in the political prison environment, and this fostered a process of 'political re-socialisation'. Some students, for example José Luís Saldanha Sanches, entering prison as members of the PCP, left prison linked to Maoism, even if not always with a specific affiliation.

The Corporate Spirit within the Academic Associations

The repression and control of the most conflictual environments also became more effective, particularly through the introduction, in all universities, of a network of informers. This was the underlying reason, together with the recruitment of young men for the Colonial War, for the increased clandestine emigration, especially to France, Switzerland and Belgium, and particularly by students and young intellectuals. At this point it should also be stressed that for the militants of the PCP this meant a choice contrary to the guidelines issued by the party, which asked young activists to enlist in the army so as to carry out propaganda and organization work within it.

Also among the institutional measures aimed at restricting student dissent were various attempts to guide the students' associative tendency towards controllable organizations. Along this line was the initiative of an alternative celebration to the Student's Day that was organized in Lisbon on 22 January 1963 named 'University Day', which, as is inferred by the name, referred more to the institution than to its members. The new Minister of National Education, Inocêncio Galvão Teles, appointed in December 1962 to replace Lopes de Almeida, whose authority had been completely compromised by the crisis, also promoted the immediate activation of the regulations established in Decree-Law 44 632, of 15 October 1962. The essence of the new legislation reproduced the proposal in 1956 with Decree-Law 40 900, which had been the pretext for the eclosion of the student unrest. An important paragraph referred to the actual structural organization of the student associations, that is, to the decision-making process *assembleias magnas* (grand meetings) open to all students.

As shown above, it was this element that conferred specificity to the type of horizontal participation conveyed by student associativism, and it was always this element that represented an unacceptable aspect to the regime due to being incompatible with the corporate nature of the state. Therefore, student bodies were accepted, but:

> Excluding everything that might suggest forms of student syndicalism imposed by the state, it was not considered less necessary to refuse legitimacy to the pretension shown by certain academic associations of becoming student syndicates, considering all the students of a university or school to be their members due to the mere fact that they are such, claiming the representativeness of all these students, even those who deliberately do not want to belong to them.[19]

Entering into the specific, through these provisions, the commissions henceforth actually controlled the student associations, whose competence and autonomy became very limited. As had already been foreseen by Decree-Law 40 900, the majority of the cultural, sports and recreational activities and the establishment of international networks required consent by the authorities, while the approval of elections for staff and the taking up office of those elected depended on the Minister of National Education himself, as did the entry into force of the statutes. The institutional response obviously went precisely in the opposite direction with respect to the demands for autonomy and self-management expressed by the great wave of student protest, as shown by the very title of the article published in *Diário de Notícias* to disclose the meaning of the new academic legislation: 'The corporate spirit within the academic associations'.[20] The statements of the Minister of National Education, Galvão Teles, went along the same lines, also always referred to in *Diário de Notícias*, which noted: 'It is important not to confuse what is university-related and what is political and above the political is the nation, of which the university is nothing but an element'.[21]

The Pluralization of the Dissident World

During the final stage of the protest cycle that I place between 1956 and 1965, there was an exceptional coexistence of many aspects of contentious politics:

crossover between old and new protest repertoires; ideologies (democratic, Catholic, socialist, communist and Maoist) and actors (students, workers and soldiers). The protest cycle, in addition to interacting with institutional politics in various ways, renovated and radically transformed Portuguese contentious politics, creating new actors and new repertoires, as well as new networks and resources – these, however, would overlap with the old ones for some time. Sometimes, new topics, determined by history itself, would change the conflictual dimension, as was the case of the Colonial War.

One of the organizations that emerged after the crisis of 1962 was the Movimento de Acção Revolucionária (Revolutionary Action Movement, MAR), created later that year by the main leaders of the crisis, including Medeiros Ferreira, Manuel de Lucena and Vasco Pulido Valente. The MAR was an organization that, in spite of its name, presented itself as more moderate than the PCP, with which, however, close relations were kept. The MAR linked itself to the Christian-humanist magazine *O Tempo e o Modo*, founded in 1963 and legally published. Since the beginning, the magazine had mobilized Catholics who were critical of the regime, such as João Benard da Costa and Adérito Sedas Nunes, and rapidly spread to other sectors of the left-wing opposition from the MUDJ, such as Mário Soares, Salgado Zenha and the then communist Sotomayor Cardia. In 1963, Salazar himself asked the PIDE/DGS to provide him with information on the magazine, having received this answer: 'It is said to be a magazine of progressive Catholics, but the list of collaborators shows that some are excessively progressive, touching the limits of communism. The director, António Alçada Baptista, offers no guarantee of cooperation in the accomplishment of the higher purposes of the state'.[22]

From 1964 onwards, the magazine increasingly addressed university topics, and by the end of the 1960s, under the influence of 'May 1968', it turned towards the left, with the collaboration of various communist sectors and future socialists, to such an extent that, from 1970 onwards, it included many important personalities of the Maoist opposition, such as Saldanha Sanches. The contacts of the MAR were also developed in other directions, with several of its representatives being present at the December 1962 meeting held in Prague by the Conference of Portuguese Anti-fascist Forces, during which the decision was made to create the Frente Patriótica de Libertação Nacional (Patriotic National Liberation Front, FPLN). The anti-fascist forces that attended this meeting, more or less directly linked to the university mobilization, were the Independent National Movement (Movimento Nacional Independente, MNI) created by General Delgado, the Republican and Socialist Resistance (Resistência Republicana e Socialista, RRS), created by Mário Soares in 1953, and the PCP. This eclecticism is particularly indicative of the political fluidity in the midst of the opposition of these years. The FPLN was initially placed in the network of communist-inspired Juntas de Acção Patriótica (Patriotic Action Councils, JAP) before establishing itself in Algeria. The organization's initial programme, as expressed in its news bulletin, especially in an article in August 1964 entitled 'Organization and unitary struggle', considered the unity of democratic and anti-fascist forces. It then pronounced itself a defender of the interests of the workers and middle classes, but through openly conflictual instruments: 'In order to destroy the machinery of the fascist State and institute democratic order, the FPLN chose the path of armed popular insurrection and alliance in the anti-fascist fight of the armed people and patriotic military personnel'.[23]

An important figure in this organization from 1964 onwards was one of the main student leaders of Coimbra, Manuel Alegre, who, based in Algiers, started to direct the radio broadcast Voz da Liberdade (Voice of Liberty), one of the principal vehicles of the opposition, which attentively followed all the events of the student movement. Humberto Delgado also moved away from the FPLN in 1964, starting up the ephemeral experience of the Portuguese National Liberation Front, with the same siglum of 'FPLN'. However, this was an organization whose plans soon proved to be rather vague and improbable, contributing to isolate the General who, in 1965, fell into an ambush in Spain, where he was killed together with his secretary.

On the socialist front, the Acção Socialista Portuguesa (Portuguese Socialist Action, ASP) was created in Geneva in 1964, especially through the initiative of Mário Soares who was in contact with around fifty militants inside Portugal. This organization would later flow into the Socialist Party, founded in Bonn in 1973.[24] Also from the Catholic side, particularly from the end of the 1960s onwards, there was a certain activism that led to the flourishing of new organizations alongside the historical and official ones such as the JUC and CADC. The main field of non-Marxist opposition, but to which it was actually quite close, was the growing Catholic opposition since the crisis of 1962, giving rise to its magazine O Tempo e o Modo that would follow, in various forms, the complex ideological path of the Portuguese dissidence.

Many of the non-Catholic organizations were formed by people who had passed through the PCP. The first Marxist–Leninist split within the PCP occurred in Paris in 1963 through the initiative of Francisco Martins Rodrigues. After a series of conflicts inside the PCP, due to which he had been removed from the Executive Committee, Martins Rodrigues was sent to Paris, still as a member of the Central Committee. As stated by Pacheco Pereira, it was there that 'Francisco Martins Rodrigues heard the discussions among exiled compatriots who disagreed with the party line relative to the Colonial War. It was here that he found an effervescent political environment moulded not only by the Sino-Soviet conflict, but also by the victorious experience of the Algerian and

Cuban revolutions' (Pacheco Pereira 2008: 163). It would be in this environment that Martin Rodrigues began to draw up the political lines of the new
movement in November–October 1963, where the themes of prior debates
inside the party converge. The outcome was the compilation of three documents, although the one that most definitively marked his rupture with the
PCP was 'Luta Pacifica e Luta Armada no Nosso Movimento', in which, apart
from insisting on the revolutionary role of the colonial liberation movements,
Martins Rodrigues affirmed the need for an armed struggle. The document
was sent, signed with the pseudonym 'Campos', to the senior structures of the
PCP, which, in December of that same year, expelled Martins Rodrigues without mentioning as justification any reference to his pro-Chinese theses, merely
pointing to disciplinary causes. Following this, the FAP was created in Paris in
March 1964, with the participation of militants from student movements – Rui
d'Espiney, João Pulido Valente, Humberto Belo and Manuel Claro, among
others. They began to publish the news bulletin *Acção Popular* in June. The
CMLP was founded in April–May, as stated by Pacheco Pereira 'within the
classic Dimitrovian conception of Party-Front relationship', where in this case
the 'front preceded the party' (Pacheco Pereira 2008: 167–68). The CMLP
began to publish *Revolução Popular*, which presented, as argued by Miguel
Cardina, 'some of the fundamental texts for the ideological definition of the
Marxist–Leninist movement' (Cardina 2011: 45–46). Unlike future Maoist
organizations that were primarily student based (tertiary sector workers
were an expanding presence), the FAP/CMLP was quite heterogeneous, with
militants from various professions.

The FAP/CMLP had a short life. Intending to install the management
of the organization in Portugal, Pulido Valente and Manuel Claro illegally
returned to the country at the end of 1964, but after the imprisonment of
various members of the organization, they went back to Paris and started to
prepare a fresh entry into Portugal together with Martins Rodrigues. Pulido
Valente was the first to re-enter the country in March 1965, while Manuel
Claro and Martins Rodrigues would pass the frontier in June. With extremely
scarce logistic and financial means, the FAP, in Portugal, was most successful
in student environments, which were still suffering from the wave of repression
in the wake of the crisis of 1962 and from the imprisonment of four leaders
of the PCP. The actions of armed struggle in the country were limited to a
few Molotov cocktails thrown against a public security police station and the
PIDE school, since, as Cardina states, 'the organization was unable to extend
its influence beyond a small core of militants and sympathizers' (Cardina 2011:
48). João Pulido Valente was imprisoned by the PIDE/DGS in October 1965,
which was followed by the arrest of ten other militants, and, in 1966, Martins
Rodrigues himself was imprisoned.

The consequences of the first split were perhaps unexpected, particularly in terms of the proliferation, by the end of the decade, of Marxist–Leninist organizations, each claiming to be a faithful reflection of the original thought, and accusing the others of being imposters and allies of the capitalist bourgeoisie. This subsequent evolution of the process of political radicalization also occurred at the time of the most profound shake up of political opportunities and pluralization of the opposition forces that led to the end of the regime, coinciding with the Marcelist period from 1969 onwards.

Notes

1. *Diário de Notícias*, 7 November 1956.
2. http://www.cadc.pt/CADCUmSculodeHistria.htm
3. Report of the Deputy Head of the Army Staff, General António Augusto dos Santos, 13 November 1970, in the Arquivo Histórico Militar (Military Historical Archive, AHM), section 40, box 1, document 4.
4. This research led to the publication by Grupo de Trabalho Português do Projecto Regional do Mediterrâneo (1963).
5. According to Casimiro Amado, the doctrine of the single school essentially consists of an expression of the key principles arising from the French Revolution towards 'maximum efficiency' in the use of national resources (cf. Amado 1998: 87).
6. McAdam, Tarrow and Tilly basically define two spaces within a specific regime, namely the political and outside the political. In the political space, the area of the government's agents is distinguished from the area of the political agents, where the latter are people who, while not being part of the government, have direct and continuous access to the government's agents and its resources. The area outside politics is composed of challengers – political actors who do not have the same opportunities as political agents or other individuals who are not organized as political actors (cf. McAdam, Tarrow and Tilly 2001: 12).
7. *Diário de Notícias*, 19 May 1962.
8. Ibid.
9. This finding is based on the analysis of the Political Prisoners File of the PIDE/DGS Archive, which, apart from the biographic details of the prisoners also includes a brief prison history, indicating, for example, punishments received and periods of sickness spent at the infirmary.
10. *Diário de Notícias*, 13 June 1962, pp. 1 and 9.
11. Ibid.
12. According to the PIDE/DGS Political Prisoners File, the prisoners were José Manuel Mendonça de Oliveira Bernardino, José Alves Tavares Magro, Manuel Álvaro Estanqueiro Nunes, João António Honrado and Alberto Ferreira Lindolfo (source: IAN/TT, Political Prisoners File of the PIDE/DGS Archive).
13. 1962 was the year with the second most student arrests (122 arrests and 153 imprisonments, where various students were arrested more than once) after 1973, when, as noted above, there were 209 student arrests 211 imprisonments (source: IAN/TT, Political Prisoners File of the PIDE/DGS Archive).

14. *Binómio*, the news bulletin of the IST and one of the most important publications of the student movement created at this very time, dedicated its first number, issued on 4 November 1964, entirely to these arrests and to the denouncement of the conditions of the imprisoned students. All the numbers of the bulletin up to 15 November 1965 – a total of 20 – were likewise dedicated to this subject.

15. *Diário de Notícias*, 11 December 1964.

16. Ibid.

17. Luís Saldanha Sanches had been delivered to the Directorate-General of the PIDE/DGS of Lisbon by the public security police on 29 April 1964 due to subversive activities and, since he was wounded during his capture, he was immediately interned in the hospital where he remained for a fortnight, after which he was transferred to Caxias prison. Taken to trial on 10 December 1964, he was sentenced to five months of correctional prison, in fact already expired with his preventative detention, and so he was released on that same day. He was captured again, this time by the actual PIDE/DGS on 18 December 1965, due to activity against the State, and once again entered Caxias prison. His second trial was held on 26 July 1966 when he was condemned to a sentence of three years of long-term imprisonment, the suspension of political rights for fifteen years, and security measures of internment of six months up to three years, extendable. On 2 November 1966, he was transferred to Peniche where he started serving the security measures on 18 December 1968. Released on 18 December 1971, yet again, on 16 May 1973, he was delivered to the Directorate-General of the PIDE/DGS of Lisbon by the public security police, again due to activity against the State, leaving on 10 July of that same year on bail. However, three weeks later he was recaptured by the public security police, and began his fourth imprisonment in Caxias, which ended on 25 April 1974.

18. *Diário de Notícias*, 22 January 1965.

19. Ibid.

20. *Diário de Notícias*, 29 January 1963.

21. Ibid.

22. PIDE/DGS report on the MUDJ, 5 February 1963, in IAN/TT-PIDE/DGS-SC-CI(1)-211-1176, folio 159.

23. 'Organization and unitary fight', the initial programme of the FPLN, August 1964.

24. Another formation had been founded in Geneva in 1970 by various exiled people (including students, former leaders of the MAR such as Medeiros Ferreira and Manuel de Lucena, and a former PCP militant, António Barreto) and would later enter the Socialist Party (PS): the Revolutionary Socialist Group (Grupo Socialista Revolucionário, GSR), which started to publish the magazine *Polémica* in 1970.

Chapter 3

'The Marcelo's Spring' and the Opening of a Second Protest Cycle

Marcelism

Continuity in Change

During the month of September 1968, following an accident in which he lost his mental faculties, Salazar had to be replaced in the position that he had held for over thirty-five years, and the President of the Republic, Américo Tomás, appointed Marcelo Caetano, out of the other possible successors, to the Presidency of the Council. The last phase of the New State was thus waved in, whose very nature, distinguishing it from the Salazarist period, is still questioned by researchers. This is especially true with respect to the 'reformist sincerity' of Marcelo Caetano, who inaugurated his term of office with promising declarations of a certain political liberalization. According to the political scientist Manuel de Lucena, the liberalization measures that Caetano effectively promulgated were motivated above all by the requirements of development, which needed the active participation of citizens. Therefore, the 'exercise of freedoms would finally be linked to the consolidation of order, instead of disturbing it', and 'Caetano's liberalization aimed at nothing more than a domesticated pluralism' (de Lucena 1995: 185).

In turn, the historian Fernando Rosas stresses that the many questions and issues concerning what Marcelism actually represented, sometimes forget that in reality Marcelism was, before and after Marcelo's grasp of power, '[a]n informal party, a reformist current inside the New State that gradually, in the wake of the Second World War, grew around Marcelo Caetano with sympathizers in sectors of the situationist political elites, economic elites, diplomatic and military corridors' (Rosas and Aires Oliveira 2004: 11).

Once in power, Marcelo Caetano embarked upon a series of social and political reforms. The most profound dimensions of the programme were those more directly linked to the industrial and economic development of the country, which included reforms or draft reforms aimed at qualifying labour and training in Portugal, as well as the country's integration in

Europe. However, the regime did venture on some opening in the political arena and in the field of labour relations, dictated especially by concerns of portraying 'winds of change' and a certain 'political relaxation'. Along these lines were the measures curbing censorship, aimed at restricting the arbitrariness of the political police, and consent of some pluralism in the single party, as well as measures that pointed to some syndicate freedom. Based on these premises, on 24 November, through the Decree-Law 49 401, the government replaced the PIDE with the DGS, although this change of name was to bring in no effective alteration to the role or repression duties of the political police. The replacement in 1970 of the single party, the UN, by the Acção Nacional Popular (National Popular Action, ANP) was similarly a mere 'cosmetic' operation.

The syndicate area was perhaps the one where the measures of opening were earliest and most advanced. An order dated 19 February 1969, sent to all heads of the police force and civil governors, stated that 'the maintenance of discipline in companies was primarily the responsibility of the entrepreneurs' (Patriarca 2008: 126). It was therefore established that strikes and other irregularities in the provision of labour did not determine immediate police intervention, and that this could only occur at the request of the employer. This was an important change, considering that previously, after the introduction of Decree-Law 23 870 in 1934, striking was considered a crime subject to a prison sentence of one year for the strikers, and many more for the organizers. Another opening in the syndicate sphere went towards eliminating the requirement for elected directors to be ratified by the Minister of Corporations. The adoption of this order arrived after a period of social calm, but coincided with an outbreak of unexpected and profound unrest in the industrial belt of Lisbon and Setúbal. The possibility cannot be excluded that the new syndicate legislation was linked to this outbreak of dissidence, in the search for a solution that did not simply rely on the police. On the other hand, among the effects of this syndicate opening, which were, as noted above, the most profound reforms of the Marcelist period, the most important would perhaps be the conquering of the boards of national syndicates by figures of the opposition, and a spectacular increase in strike action, which also lost its almost exclusively worker-based nature (Patriarca 2004: 173).

Here, it became evident, as other authors have already emphasized (Palacios Cerezales 2011), Marcelism was a clear example of the opening of political opportunities. However, the Marcelist opening was not linear, but in part took a step backwards in reaction to the great wave of mobilizations that accompanied it. In the meantime, this closure could achieve little at a time when a large part of society was showing signs of a profound dislike of the regime. Thus, in 'lifting the lid', the regime discovered that it faced a real 'pressure pan', in a process where 'factors started to play a preponderant role, such as the driving energy of the awakened forces, the pressure of alliances that were circumstantial but of a wider ambition, or external constraints and interferences' (Rosas and Aires Oliveira 2004: 13). As indeed noted by Fátima Patriarca:

> The reforms of 1969 should not be underestimated. They created high expectations, from the top to the bottom of society. And they also created a mechanism of change and new spaces, which led to a perception of Marcelism as different from Salazarism. But this opening also fostered a heightening of social pressure, which had already begun to be visible in the late 1960s. Society changed, from its habits to ideologies, as did the relations of social forces ... The combination of the reforms and social pressure created dynamics that the state had difficulty in overcoming. The State fluctuated between opening and closure, which was to become the riskiest of policies. (Patriarca 2004: 205)

In fact, the regime and its institutions, above all those of public security, were not prepared to sustain a legitimization of social conflict, even if marginal, to face the different facets of the movements in a flexible manner. This led to the frustrations of expectations held by the movements, which relative to the more sensitive issues merely received a repressive response, causing the re-closure of previously granted openings, especially because it proved to be impossible to liberalize while keeping open what was becoming the main axis of the conflict, that is, the Colonial War (Hammond 1988; Costa Pinto 2001).

However, no closure could place the lid back on the social forces that had been unleashed with the opening. On the other hand, by ignoring this 'collective effervescence' it is difficult to understand the exceptional mobilization that distinguished the first phase of the Portuguese transition. The following chapters will, therefore, describe the process underlying the formation of the unexpected political radicalization that distinguished the revolutionary period towards the end of the regime.

Spring in the Institutions

In fact, more than Caetano's actual affirmations, particularly those expressed in his inaugural speech upon taking office in his new position, were the statements of some of his colleagues which could be considered as 'bolder' in a reformist perspective. For example, as Rita Almeida de Carvalho recalls, it was the new Minister of the Interior, Gonçalves Rapazote, who, although considered a hardliner of the regime, stated in public that Marcelism should be a 'political spring' (Almeida de Carvalho 2004: 36). Even more explicit were the words of the new President of the Executive Committee of the National Union, Guilherme de Melo e Castro, which suggested an adaptation of the regime to the model of West European political systems (ibid.). On the other hand, it was this opening at the highest levels of the National Union that contributed to thickening the ranks of his so-called 'Liberal Wing'.

The origin of the Liberal Wing should be sought in the context of the succession of Salazar by Caetano and 'in his premeditated activity in creating a support group within the National Assembly' (Fernandes 2006: 68). However, its roots had already been the outcome of the changes in relations between the New State and the Church during the two previous decades, and its attraction resided above all in the Catholic doctrine developed by the Second Vatican Council (ibid.: 69). The Liberal Wing would represent the institutional crowning of the process of autonomization of Catholic associativism relative to the corporate structures, although this group would above all be used by the regime to give a 'veneer of political respectability in the eyes of the international community' and, at an internal level, to 'distance itself from the most conservative factions of the regime' (ibid.: 21).

The use of the Liberal Wing as a facade for Caetano's policy is confirmed by the fact that the proposals it submitted towards an attenuation of the authoritarian characteristics of the regime were never approved. These proposals particularly referred to draft reviews of constitutional law, with a return to the direct election of the President of the Republic, to amnesty for political prisoners, to judicial reorganization and to freedom of press, religious and associative activity. The parliamentary obstructionism to these projects eventually led to the Liberal Wing leaving the National Assembly and its representatives' decision not to re-candidate in the elections of 1973. However, their exclusion from this area of the government evidently did not imply the disappearance of the social block, especially of Catholic nature, which the Liberal Wing represented. The Liberal Wing thus shifted from its semi-opposition angle to a position of real political opposition, contributing to the climate of polarization that would be the distinctive mark of the last years of the regime. Many Catholics passed definitively over to the opposition, considering that an approximation to the radical environments of political dissent, even of Marxist affiliation, was more viable than alignment with the regime. The Colonial War was obviously not unrelated to this process, especially from the early 1970s onwards, with the expulsion of various Catholic orders such as the Combonian Fathers and White Fathers from the colonies, and the progressive international awareness of the crimes of the Portuguese army. Pope Paul VI's reception, in 1970, of Marcelino dos Santos and other leaders of the liberation movements merely confirms this line, and marked the significantly growing gap between many Catholic sectors and the regime.

Veiga Simão, Minister of National Education

One of the directions of the reformist path of the Caetano government of most interest from the perspective of the present study, due to its implications in student mobilization processes, was the education reform project, whose implementation had been held off for many years. As will be shown further below, the situation of institutional debate was replayed around a topic of direct interest to the students, and this contributed, as it had at the beginning of the 1960s, to provide resources and open opportunities for student mobilization.

As highlighted by Maria Cândida Proença (2004), throughout the entire 1960s, and under the influence of the increased compulsory education introduced by Leite Pinto, the most important phenomenon in the field of education was the growing demand for instruction. However, this measure, due to the material and organizational lacunae in education, not only produced a rise in school attendance, but also a lowering of quality. Moreover, in spite of the affirmation of the principles of a single school, a clear discrimination was maintained in distinguishing between students who intended to pursue their education and those who decided to enter work directly.

Notwithstanding this restrictive policy, the demand for secondary education increased greatly in preparatory cycles which enabled entrance into university, with the effect of a heavy disorganization of education at this level. One of the consequences of this situation was the exponential increase in private education, which soon actually exceeded public education in quantitative terms. This situation, and the conflicts that it created and could create, was the underlying reason for Caetano's decision to implement changes that could, on the one hand, reduce the cleavage between the development-driven aspirations of its government and the potentialities of the education system, and on the other hand, prevent and eliminate some of the motivations underlying the student unrest.

In the opinion of Maria Cândida Proença, Marcelo Caetano appointed the young José Veiga Simão to the position of Minister of National Education in 1970, one year after the serious academic crisis of 1969, 'to attempt to reverse the current situation, boost the necessary changes and establish calmer relations with the academic associations' (Proença 2004: 242). Veiga Simão, professor of physics at Coimbra University, apart from his young age, presented an international and innovative profile, due to having completed a doctorate in nuclear physics at Cambridge University and having already been Rector of General Studies in Mozambique.

Regarding the education system as a whole, two texts were disclosed on 6 June 1971 titled 'Project of the Portuguese School System' and 'General Lines of the Reform of Higher Education'. The principal lines developed by the first of these proposed increasing secondary education by a full year, unifying middle and complementary secondary education, and extinguishing special middle education. The second document addressed the restructuring of higher education, with a view to extending it to the remoter parts of the country by instituting various polytechnic schools, universities, and other more specific establishments.

Following the publication of these two documents, a public debate opened, with requests from the minister himself for contributions from all sectors potentially involved in the reform: student committees, school authorities, academic associations, to quote but a few. The preparatory work of the reform was undertaken by the Education Action Planning and Research Office, organized directly under the minister. Although the law that endorsed the basis on which the reform should be conducted was only approved in July 1973, the minister was already working, between 1971 and 1973, towards implementing the measures he considered most urgent.

While the measures proposed by the reform were clearly of a progressive nature, in the currents of the opposition it was generally considered, as will be discussed below, that without a change of regime this new course in the area of education had not brought in any structural innovation. On the other hand, the reform also raised voices of dissent in the most conservative sectors of the actual regime, which above all contested the issue of values, principally in the religious and patriotic field, and the fact that the compulsory teaching of religious education had been eliminated. As would be seen, clearly unable to implement all the foreseen measures, the reform also led to an intense debate among various sectors of society, having indeed involved almost all the opposition factions – Catholic, communist, new-left, socialist – that showed different responses to the measures proposed by the minister. The opening favoured by the reform and the minister himself, also with a view to establishing a process of pacification, in meeting some of the most pressing demands that had, for years, been at the heart of the student protest, also led to the emergence of new requests, especially towards a general restructuring of society and the political system. The debate surrounding the reform thus contributed to politicizing the academic environments, where it was increasingly more evident that it would be very difficult to democratize education without, simultaneously, opening up a process of democratization in the country.

Mobilization Resources and Repertoire

One Step Back: The Floods of 1967

In protest cycles it is fairly common that an unexpected event contributes to confering an indelible mark on the socio-political configuration of the actors. This convergence of factors occurred at the time of the floods that greatly affected Lisbon and its surroundings in November 1967, contributing to the spreading of the politicization and mobilization of the university environment. This was both due to the fact that the floods made the students aware of the real conditions of poverty prevalent in the country, and that it provided an exceptional occasion for self-managed participation. Rather similar circumstances had also occurred in 1966 in two important Italian cities, Trento and Florence.

The Trento floods arrived at a time when student political activity was just beginning and contributed to extend the mobilization to other cities, through the students who travelled from the north of Italy to offer assistance to the affected population. The Trento floods also led to the suspension of the university's occupation which was underway, aimed at the legal recognition of the licentiate degree in sociology, which was later achieved. As the students were driven to participate in the relief work, they created ties of solidarity with the citizens. In an interview, Marco Boato, a leader of Lotta Continua, stated 'that the occupation was dissolved by the floods. One morning, we woke up, saw the water on the steps of the cathedral and went to help to remove the mud. In Trento, Florence, Venice, for our generation it was the first experience of voluntary work' (Cazzullo 2006: 27).

Similarly to the Trento floods, those that affected Florence, causing close to three hundred deaths and twelve thousand evacuated citizens, contributed to expand and politicize the mobilization, being recalled by Sidney Tarrow as an occasion, on the one hand, of discrediting the institutions and, on the other hand, of horizontal cooperation between citizens – two particularly effective conditions to motivate and extend the protest:

> The clean-up efforts begin, but the means and manpower [available] to the Florentines are hopelessly inadequate. The arrival of help from international agencies is weeks away. The government in

Rome announces the allocation of 'extraordinary' resources, but so far all that materialises are thousands of soldiers milling around in wet shoes with no one to tell them what to do. As in all emergencies, local assistance is first organized by neighbourhood groups, youth organizations and parish churches. (Seidelman 1979, in Tarrow 1989: 112)

Included among those who offered to work as volunteers to clean up the city were a number of students who had arrived from all over Italy. The political and university environment of the region was already particularly active and the city had been the stage, in 1964, of the breakaway of the magazine *Classe Operária* from the Quaderni Rossi group and would be the headquarters of the first congress of Potere Operaio in 1970. However, it was not only workerism that would characterize the Florentine political environment, since it was in this Tuscan city that the most radical Catholic dissention had developed.

It was evident that the students coming in to assist the inhabitants of Florence in dealing with the effects of the floods would easily absorb these ideas, especially considering that the organizations around which the Florentine political and social conflict agglomerated were also those that most participated in the relief (Iacuaniello, Pantano and Bollino 2009). In this perspective, it is interesting to quote the words of Francesco Bollosi, a former militant of Potere Operaio, who, in 1966 while still a high school student, travelled from the northern city of Como to Florence in order to offer help:

I was at the Paolo Giovio scientific high school, at that time the 'prestigious' school, attended by lots of boys and a few girls of the wealthy of Como ... The story began to change in November of 1966, after the Florence floods. In Florence, in the boilers of the station, we cleaned books from the 1500 and 1600s during one month. At school, they considered us truants and progressed considerably with the programme. When we returned, we were treated as irresponsible. And this sparked our rebellion. (Grandi 2003: 22)

Another testimonial, this time from Bologna, is also significant in this perspective:

When we returned to Bologna, we felt an almost physical pain in re-encountering a city with a completely regular life ... Stepping out of the bus, covered in mud from head to toe, once again back in Maggiore Square, the passersby stared at us as though we were strange and disturbing beings, while we felt heavy with feelings incommunicable to those who have not experienced them … It was a decisive experience in my life, a stage that marked the path of my entry into adulthood … I do not wish to forget, of course, the effect of the growth, also social, brought about by that experience to a generation: a very few years later I found all my friends of the Florentine journey involved in the station of the student movement. (Mazzone 2006)

In Portugal, the floods of November 1967 affected various zones of the country, but none with the severity reached in Lisbon and the Tagus valley, since this is also the most inhabited part of the country. The first estimates, in the newspaper *Diário de Notícias* dated 27 November, reported 250 deaths and dozens missing, but this calculation was fated to rise, and three days later the same newspaper reported 427 victims, a figure still far from the real number. The most affected settlements were those of the poorest, who in many cases lived in houses little better than huts. Negligence in maintaining the riverbanks had also contributed to make the situation even more dramatic, and likewise the conditions of the communication routes, which had so greatly delayed both the flight and relief (Benamor Duarte 1997: 172–74).

The real scale of the disaster and the living conditions of a vast layer of Portuguese society did not pass through the thick curtain of censorship of the regime, but many university students, who had intervened to provide immediate assistance, were able to enter into contact with the true situation. The organization of the student intervention was initially coordinated by the Catholic activists and later followed by many student associations and pro-associations of the capital, especially those with connections to the IST, one of the most active establishments since the beginning. The planning of the relief effort was entrusted to a Coordinating Central Committee installed in the student association of the IST (Cardina 2008: 64). Various initiatives were also organized at Coimbra University, such as fund-raising coordinated by the Conselho das Repúblicas (Council of the Republics, CR) – the traditional collective student residences of this city – that received the support of the CADC and all autonomous bodies, including Orfeon, normally connoted with the right wing (ibid.), while other donations arrived from Porto.

The students were particularly well placed to undertake this task, being exempt from work commitments and having an effective organization network. Furthermore, many possessed specific skills that made their intervention especially useful, above all the medical students, who conducted vaccination work and monitored the health of the affected population. The assistance provided by the students drew harsh responses from the authorities, concerned with the detailed descriptions of the real conditions of poverty and the ineffectiveness of public relief disclosed through the academic press. As noted by Marta Benamor Duarte, the participation of almost six thousand students in the relief activities did not please the authorities, who intervened seeking to hinder and discredit this work, including through the use of the public security police (Benamor Duarte 1997). In turn, Miguel Cardina emphasizes that on various occasions the Council of the Republics denounced the fact that the authorities systematically censored the news relative to the student-organized solidarity campaign (Cardina 2008: 64).

In any case, the most important aspect concerning these episodes was the spread and expansion of student participation beyond the traditional channels of academic engagement and outside the narrow perimeter of the university campus. Also in this case, as in Florence and Trento, the principal component of the organization of the intervention was its self-management, and this was the first episode of this type experienced by a large number of students. As Cardina notes, the students' participation, in spite of their feelings of impotence in view of the magnitude of the tragedy for which they were unprepared, gave them an opportunity to criticize the failings of the government's health and social services, to show the effectiveness of democratically organized bodies (such as the student support network) and to denounce the miserable living conditions in various parts of the country (Cardina 2008). Equally important was the simultaneous effort of providing information and reporting, for which new magazines were even created, such as *Solidariedade Social*. This activity was reflected, in many cases, in actual reporting with interviews of the inhabitants of the affected zones and detailed documentation on the 'real country'.

From various points of view, this work ran along similar lines to what was burgeoning in Italy through the different counter-information surveys, radios and magazines. Moreover, for many students, the campaign definitively marked a breakaway from the New State. The student militant João Bernardo, who was banned from all universities of the country for an undefined period, also recalls the participation in the floods as a point of no return in the politicization of the Portuguese student environment (Cardina 2008: 66), while others, such as Jorge Wemans, future director of Rádio Televisão Portuguesa (Portuguese Radio Television, RTP), testified above all to the fact that this voluntary participation had fostered the creation of solid networks of trust and identification:

> I recall that, after the floods, when we wanted to disseminate the theses of the Aveiro Congress,[1] for any anti-colonial document, or

if considering participation in the elections of 1969, or wanting to organize a holiday camp, or any action or meeting of reflection, we would start to exchange names and telephone numbers, and then the eternal question would arise: 'But who is this guy, can he be trusted?', which would receive the inevitable answer: 'But don't you remember? He was also in the floods with us!'. Having participated in those days had become sufficient prior qualification.[2]

At that same time, the organization of so-called 'holiday camps' had begun, through which groups of students reached the most remote parts of the country to enter into contact with local populations, ministering adult literacy courses and participating in community work (see Cardina 2008: 67). Moreover, these incursions into the very heart of Portugal served to deepen awareness of traditions and popular culture, quite apart from the reinventions that had been designed by the regime over the years. These practices were real innovations in the repertoire of mobilization of civil society, at this time driven by students, destined to be institutionalized after the fall of the regime, during the PREC, in the context of the 'Cultural dynamization campaign' organized by the MFA and Student Civic Service (Tiago de Oliveira 2004).

It is more difficult to ascertain the position of the PCP relative to this student mobilization, aimed at providing assistance to the population affected by the floods. There is indeed little documentation on the issue, although the party's official press suggests an attitude rather more directed at denouncing the State's responsibilities than at preventing disaster, both in terms of any relief offered after the event and support of solidarity initiatives. The party's underground news bulletin *Avante!* indicates that Salazar did not even decree national mourning, which had even been declared on the occasion of Hitler's death. Furthermore, the government was denounced for not attributing special funds for reconstruction, and essentially for having based its actual intervention primarily on private generosity:

What does the government do after the tragedy? What does it consider doing? … It appointed heartless fascists and high society ladies to the tasks of assistance, that is, for the collection of donations and their distribution … The government's expenditure in assistance to the victims is primarily based on the collection of donations, on the widespread solidarity movement which the tragedy provoked on a national and world scale. Not a single special budget allocation. Not even a single serious, meditated and timely measure to swiftly deal with the most pressing needs.[3]

Also denounced was the fact that many people who had tried to intervene directly to provide assistance had been turned away, but the emphasis of the PCP's discourse primarily concentrated on its appeal to all workers, peasants, young people and, more in general, democrats, to 'intensify their acts of solidarity to the victims of the recent tragedy, accompanying and supporting those in diligences and actions of protest, so that their demands are swiftly met, so that the state should pay for the abuses and damages resulting from its own policies'.[4]

It is evident that this position, apart from having different consequences on the mobilization processes, contrasted completely with the self-management line chosen by the student organizations. The differences between the historical left and the new movements became clearly visible in this situation: on the one side, the PCP called for greater public interventions, an expansion and higher efficacy of the state's duties, accusing the regime of being quite insufficient in this sense; on the other side, the emerging movements contested the ineffectiveness of the public services, but based their action on self-organization aimed at replacing the state in the management of social life.

This point appears to be very significant in the gradually larger cleavage between the Communist Party and the student movement, which would be increasingly deeper from the late 1960s onwards. Therefore, on the one hand, an efficient structure of self-management started to evolve, alongside the development of the traditional channels of antagonist activism, such as the PCP; on the other hand, a very large number of people had been mobilized who would not easily return back to the ranks of rigid academic discipline once the emergency was over. This is hardly surprising considering that, after this experience, the students' return to university would coincide with the beginning of 1968, a year that propelled national youth contestation into the higher arena of a worldwide movement.

The Students of the IST Decree a Sexual Revolution

By the end of the 1960s, the Portuguese student movement was thus entering a new phase, strongly influenced by factors of internal politics (e.g. Marcelism and the rekindling of the Colonial War), external politics such as May 1968, and unexpected events such as the floods of 1967. By the first months of 1968 there appeared to be a stronger politicization of student environments, whose most significant episode was the holding in February of the first demonstration in Portugal against the Vietnam War, conducted by students who were soon to be among the founding members of the Esquerda Democrática Estudantil (Student Democratic Left, EDE), which will be discussed in the next chapter. This politicization would further intensify over the following months and years. Hence, although the most recalled event of the late 1960s is the crisis of 1969, in fact there were a series of conflictual actions in the universities or triggered by students since December 1968, when the Minister of Education reported the presence of a 'small group of agitators' in Lisbon universities who incited the students against the authorities and who primarily came, once again, from the corridors of the IST.

On 8 December 1968, the MEN decided to resort to the early closing of the IST and the suspension of all the associative leaders of this institution. The motivations alleged by the MEN resided in a situation defined as the 'upscale' of the student conflict, whose most notable episodes were detailed as the holding of the Protest Song Festival at the IST on 26 October, with the presentation of songs and poems of authors considered 'communists', and the calling of a demonstration on 31 October, in the Praça do Comércio, to protest against the death, in Caxias prison, of the student Daniel Teixeira.[5]

Other decisive moments of the conflict upscale were the major movement of Lisbon students to Coimbra to celebrate the so-called 'Taking of the Bastille'[6] on 25 November, and the occupation of Lisbon University campus on 4 December with the holding of a protest picnic. The picnic event had been accompanied by the destruction of the access doors to the women's recreational areas, with the justification that this separation was reactionary. Finally, 'subversive' members of the IST had supposedly infiltrated the faculties of Law and Letters, seeking to convince the students to join the movement, and distributing a pamphlet that stated: 'The students of the IST decree a sexual revolution and a strike with occupation of the premises'.

Albeit with a certain lack of political definition, without the clear prevalence of any particular group, but with an evident influence, for the first time, of voices most likely of the new left, the intense turmoil that swept through the IST during the last months of 1968 showed a complete renovation of the repertoire of action and themes. This evolution is fairly significant if one looks at the leading movement of the crisis of 1962, which had still employed moderate and conventional forms of action in dealing with the government to try to obtain permission to hold the Student's Day. Merely six years later, the objectives declared by the students of the IST now included a sexual revolution, the elimination of barriers between genders, while the news bulletin of the student association of the IST, *Binómio*, was no longer limited to defending the democratization of the university and society, but launched a far more radical criticism against bourgeois society and the 'inevitably' authoritarian institutions it produced such as government, school and family.[7]

The Mobilization of Coimbra

While increasingly more radical conflictual episodes were continually repeated in Lisbon, the traditional instruments of student contestation continued to be used in Coimbra at this time (Cardina 2008). Therefore, in this city the events of 1968 appeared to occur without major complications for the authorities. It is sufficient to glance through the PIDE/DGS archive folder on the conflictual activity in Coimbra University during the academic year of 1967/68 to see that, in comparison with the following years and especially 1969, there is very little material relative to conflictual events. It is also true that, since 1965, the Direcção Geral da Associação Académica de Coimbra (General Board of Coimbra Academic Association, DGAAC), the students' representative body, had been secured by an Administrative Commission of a non-elective nature, and that the mobilization that would characterize the year 1969 would arise precisely against this situation. The fact that Coimbra University was experiencing a relatively calm period even following the loss of autonomy of its academic association tells us a lot about the importance of these academic bodies in the organization and management of the conflictual activity at the university, as logistical, ideological and human resources.

On the other hand, the absence of this form of legal representation of the students contributed, here as in other cases, to the constitution of an alternative network that was more informal and partly underground, and therefore less controllable by the authorities, which was organized around the circuit of the Republics (Repúblicas), that is, the traditional student residences of Coimbra. It is important to note that, of the twenty-three republics, except for the 'Chinese Pagoda', considered monarchical, all were adverse to the regime and considered themselves 'ruled by democratic processes of management'.[8] Furthermore, the republics were in themselves a remarkable network of mobilization, endowed with an efficient organization constituted by the CR, whose executive body was its secretariat. The CR also published a news bulletin, *O Badalo*, which would be of considerable importance in the successive phases of contestation. In fact, the great majority of the autonomous bodies of Coimbra Academic Association were considered against the regime, such as the Teatro dos Estudantes Universitário de Coimbra (Coimbra University Student Theatre, TEUC) and the CITAC.

In an explicit manner, after a clearly reactionary past and a long phase of ambiguity, the CADC was also considered against the regime.[9] By 1967, the headquarters of the CADC had been the stage of conferences of members of the oppositionist magazines *Seara Nova* and *O Tempo e o Modo*, in which, as reported by the PIDE/DGS, an 'apologia of the autonomy of the university' had been expressed, also appealing to the fight against the regime. Student pressure towards the holding of elections for the General Board of the DGAAC had begun by 1967, with a petition also supported by various Catholic entities. At the time, this mobilization did not appear to involve the majority of the students, although it is possible to perceive in it a first budding of future unrest that would also be influenced by the institutional opening offered by the change of Prime Minister.

The Inspector of the PIDE/DGS, Jorge Alegria Leite de Faria, denounced that if subservient initiatives were successful, this was primarily because the administrative commissions imposed by the government, in replacement of the freely elected DGAAC, had not developed any work towards attempting to involve and stimulate the students:

> In all fairness, one must recognize, unfortunately, the apathy and lack of initiative, the insufficiency of the administrative commissions that will surely weigh heavily on the spirit of most students, even if politically indifferent, when they should express their opinion on the convenience of elections for the AAC. It would hardly be strange if, in the near future, a pro-election commission were to achieve its intention: academic unrest, which would be used to the full advantage of the party.[10]

In fact, this underground mobilization around the holding of new elections for the DGAAC did not employ particularly transgressive tactics, but, judging from the scale of the protest that involved the university during the following year, it was very effective and managed to attract a large number of students, who were also moderate and, to use the words of the PIDE/DGS, 'politically indifferent'. For example, on 25 November 1967, on the occasion of the commemoration of the 'Taking of the Bastille', the Council of the Republics had managed to ensure that the procession would be transformed into a silent march, with one thousand students walking in an absolutely ordered form along the city's streets. In the beginning of 1968, this same council created a pro-elections commission that proposed to interact with the academic authorities, exerting pressure to approve free elections. The CADC, the TEUC, the CITAC, the Choir, the Mixed Choir and the Tuna Académica[11] all joined this action, with the exception of Orfeon, of national tendencies, which kept clear of the initiative.[12]

In May, the rector was thus given a petition with two thousand signatures requesting the holding of the elections. However, the new circumstances of the country, that would be swept in soon after the appointment of Marcelo Caetano to the Presidency of the Council on 27 September 1968, led to a new opening at an institutional level, whose consequences, in terms of mobilization, were rapidly understood by the political police: 'In view of the recent events that have taken place in the country and having observed a greater freedom of expression of the media channels, namely the press, the students of the left are showing their delight at what they consider a promising opening, failing to conceal their great expectations of a thorough and radical transformation of academic politics'.[13]

A petition was in fact sent to the new President of the Council to favour the holding of academic elections, and on 2 November this request received a positive response. From this moment onwards, practically all student activity was dedicated to the organization of the elections and to the electoral campaign. At this same time, the topic of the academic reform announced by the new minister, Veiga Simão, was included in the issues of the student mobilization of Coimbra. The delegates of the Council of the Law Faculty thus drew up a document to define the students' positions in relation to the reform projects. This document sought to compile the suggestions of each course relative to various subjects, addressing logistic, organization and specifically pedagogic issues. Pedagogic issues primarily implied changes in the form of teaching: small classes, abolition of truancy notes, abolition of the aptitude exam, exams in March, abolition of the exam charge, reorganization of the teacher recruitment system and permanent scientific updating. Finally, there was a series of demands of a representative nature, such as recognition of all student representation bodies, and participation of the students in the School Council and in the University Senate.[14] All these aspects pointed to a greater democratization of education, whether in relation to the broadening of university in terms of access to education, or in relation to student participation in academic decisions.

As was the case in 1962, the institutional debates on educational reform were immediately reflected in the sphere of contentious politics. The actual PIDE/DGS noted that 'the issues linked to the elections are added to those linked to the government discussion on the university reform'.[15] Hence, topics related to the reform of education that up to then had not shown any political veneer and were even favoured by the majority of the students and various teachers, were taken up by the Council of the Republics, which, according to the authorities, appeared to seek to 'confer a political nature to the issue, insisting on including it in a series of demands'.[16]

The Academic Crisis of Coimbra

The elections for the new leaders of the Academic Association were finally held on 12 February 1969 and, according to the PIDE/DGS report, of the 2,069 enrolled members, 1,524 voted for the list of the Council of the Republics and 455 voted for the other. The percentage was 73.7% against 22.9%, plus 3.25% of abstentions.[17] This not only represented a major victory for the list of the left wing, but also a great victory for associative freedoms and student representation within the university, which had returned after three years of abolition. The activism of the students linked to the pro-election commission and Council of the Republics had been particularly fundamental in ensuring this success.

With this renewed legal representation, the student movement of Coimbra was now able to organize itself and expand, involving the majority of the students in the crisis that was brewing. In fact, what most distinguished the academic conflict of Coimbra in 1969 was clearly the massive mobilization of students, which reached its peak on 17 April when, on the occasion of the visit of President of the Republic Américo Tomás to inaugurate the new Mathematics facilities, the student Alberto Martins, prevented from speaking during the celebration, openly questioned the Head of State. This was followed by violent police repression which fell on the student demonstration that had gathered around the new building and would continue along the streets of the city.[18]

In the meantime, the students occupied the amphitheatre and 17 April was declared 'Day of the Science Faculty'.[19] In the version of the facts disclosed in Lisbon, by the news bulletin of the Instituto Superior de Ciências Económicas e Financeiras (Higher Institute of Economics and Management, ISCEF), it was noted that the President of the Republic had responded positively to Alberto Martins' request to speak, but that he had not respected the promise. Hence, close to two hundred students present 'burst out in screams for freedom and democracy'[20] while the room was invaded by the PIDE/DGS, who evacuated it brutally. The students then went over to the Faculty of Science, that was occupied to call a plenary meeting and, upon closing, they embarked on a silent march of protest up to the canteen where they held a meeting.

The ISCEF's news bulletin immediately portrayed the political aspects of the events, connected to the supposed Marcelist opening: 'Once again, repression was unleashed on students, proving that in spite of an announced political spring, the government does not hesitate in using the many weapons it possesses against the students'.[21] A strike on classes was decreed from 17 April onwards at Coimbra University. At the same time, however, the decision was taken to submit an official apology to the President of the Republic, aimed at achieving the immediate release of the students who were still imprisoned and the establishment of an inquiry on the attitude of the police. Alberto Martins, released not long after, presided over a grand meeting (*assembleia magna*) with two thousand students, where he read the text that was intended to be submitted to the President of the Republic, which contained, apart from the apology, a description of the university atmosphere and a request to end the measures of suspension and criminal proceedings in relation to students.

This represented an attitude which, due to its aspect of 'admission of guilt', as shall be seen, raised various criticisms not only in Lisbon's student environments but also in other factions. Martins' other proposals followed along the line of Coimbra University's traditions such as the use of the university gown and cape during the visit to the President, and the main-tenance of academic mourning in Coimbra. Moreover, it is significant that these demands, in the opinion of the academic leader, should be achieved through the support of teachers and, as would later occur, of the Rector, in an attitude that was, in all senses, one of opening up dialogue with the institutions. At the same time, on the other hand, at a grand meeting on 8 May, the students decided on the continuation of academic mourning through strike action during the exam period.

Political Process and Protest

Historiography generally refers to the Coimbra academic crisis of 1969 as the most symbolic and important event of the student opposition of the final years of the regime.[22] However, it was arguably just one of the phases of the ongoing conflictual attitude in the universities that characterized the last years of the regime and all university cities. On this issue, Miguel Cardina notes:

> The first common point consists of the appraisal of the 'academic crises' as the crucial moment of student activism. In doing so, one falls into a type of episodic history, based on a rather euphemistic key concept, albeit used at the time, both by the students, as a manner of calling attention to the contestation that they led, and by the government, which thus enabled reducing the unrest to 'natural normality'. In the last analysis, placing the emphasis on the 'academic crises' does not facilitate the understanding of the deep process of political, social and cultural dissidence that swept through the student territory during these years. (Cardina 2008: 204)

It would appear that not only do the internal evolutive elements of the actual student movement considered by Cardina contrast with an analysis concentrated excessively on moments of crisis, but also that this movement, and others likewise, needs to be contextualized and studied in terms of its relationship with long-term dynamics and political processes.

Marta Benamor Duarte suggests four underlying reasons behind the unrest of 1969, some of which have already been referred to above in relation to the mobilizations in Lisbon at the end of 1968. These four elements primarily include the replacement of Salazar by Caetano and the consequent Marcelist Spring. Secondly, there was the death of the student Daniel Teixeira in Caxias prison which occupied the news bulletins of Lisbon's main student associations for days on end, together with the denouncement of the true nature of the regime and falsity of the Marcelist change. Thirdly, in terms of actual education policy, there was the university reform project. The fourth and last factor was the normalization of the associative life of Lisbon's Faculty of Science and Coimbra University, where administrative commissions appointed by the government had been enforced since 1965. However, this implied that the situations of some institutes which had literally been deprived of their associations still needed to be resolved, which was the case of the Faculty of Medicine, the Faculty of Letters, and the Higher School of Fine Arts of Lisbon. The imminent intervention of the institutions to settle the situation, instead of calming down the students, created new tensions, fostering further mobilization. In the student environment, there was good reason to believe that the adopted measures had gone in a direction rather different to that demanded by the interested parties.

The constellation of political opportunities was, therefore, once again particularly favourable to mobilization. Firstly, while Marcelism had not in fact imposed structural modification to the regime, its actual establishment had represented a break in institutional continuity. In the second place, as in 1962, a rather heated debate was underway among the elites that opened or reopened issues left hanging, and concerning which the government was planning an intervention. The university reform was one such issue and the students immediately demonstrated their justified fear that the government would take initiatives without their participation. Hence, in view of the government debate, by November 1968, a joint statement of the student associations of Lisbon reported that the planned alterations would not be accepted unless they provided for all the rights that had been denied up to this date, which was a possibility that, on the other hand, the students suspected might actually occur.

The interest shown by the regime was interpreted simply as the result of a change in the government's internal balances, under the weight of new economic and social interests, and therefore totally unrelated to the effective demands of the students. This was precisely the core issue of the protest: any exploitation of the university for economic or political interests was radically rejected; in other words, the students repudiated the actual idea, underlying the discussion between the liberal sectors of the regime, of a university that would boost the capitalist development of the country. Now, it was no longer merely a criticism of the educational backwardness of Portugal that had fuelled the crisis of 1962, but a much larger contestation on the very meaning of education in society. The demand was for autonomy of the education system, with respect to the economic and political processes of the country, and the path to achieve this objective was identified in intense and ongoing work developed by the actual students within the walls of the universities, through meetings, debates, conference cycles – in short: self-management.

The Divergent Paths of Student Contestation in Coimbra and Lisbon

The Declining Phase of the Coimbra Crisis

The first signs of student demobilization in Coimbra appeared during the last phases of the strikes against exams of June 1969 that, while initially participated in by the majority, lost many of its numbers over time, especially after the MEN stated that students who had not attended previous exams would not be penalized. At this same time, the police identified the eighty-four students who had most stood out during the crisis.

As stressed by Marta Benamor Duarte, the weakness of the movement had begun to be visible from its initial confrontation with political repression, which contributed to create a split between the students in general and the associative leaders. The latter were called in by the authorities, taken to court, expelled, imprisoned or, in some cases, enlisted, leaving the movement adrift. Police incursions onto academic premises were frequent occurrences at this time, as was the patrolling of city streets by security forces, especially at night.

The first major decline in the buoyancy of the student movement arrived, however, as in many other cases, with the onset of summer and the long holiday period. This was particularly because the government took advantage of this period of low mobilization to wipe out the leaders and suspend the activities of the AAC.[23] On the other hand, since the summer of 1969, many student leaders were being called up to enlist in military service due to the new conscription law promulgated through Decree-Law 49 099.[24] The student movement was thus deprived of its means of sustenance and at the mercy of the sanctions imposed by the Ministry of Education.

The closure of the AAC, once again, eliminated the only legal space of student participation and representation of Coimbra University and, as had happened during the period of enforcement of the administrative commission, the only way for the movement to continue to exist was by retreating from the public sphere into an atmosphere of conspiracy that, once again, gathered around the republics. An official space of participation would open, however, outside the university, in the specifically political arena of the electoral campaign of the autumn of 1969, when most of the students of Coimbra decided to enrol in the lists of the Comissão Democrática Eleitoral (Electoral Democratic Commission, CDE), which will be discussed in greater detail in the following chapter.

With the resumption of the second exam period in the autumn of 1969, the movement appeared to have lost much of its former strength. In fact, the military conscription programme had wielded disastrous short-term effects on the student mobilization of Coimbra, with all of the forty-nine strongest activists of the crisis of 1969 having been recruited since the summer and forced to attend military service in Mafra. However, while the conscription of the most active students had left the academic environment of Coimbra a calmer place, this solution also led to a dangerous situation within the actual armed forces, where, from this time onwards, and even at Mafra School, there was an intensification of episodes of insubordination, such as desertion, theft of military material, and distribution of subversive propaganda.

Hence, although the PIDE/DGS was able to foresee that Coimbra University's environment would be calm in the new year, 'with the students nursing expectations concerning the new Minister of National Education',[25] it should also be stressed that 'a revolutionary action was being kindled in Mafra which had already contributed to the flight of eight students, particularly to France'. The leadership of this revolutionary action was attributed to Celso Cruzeiro, considered 'the most dangerous associative member to have entered in this conscription'.[26] In general, compulsory military service became a key channel to disseminate subversive ideas within the ranks of the armed forces. All students, dissidents or otherwise, were obliged to join the military, and only a minority were able to evade the draft. The testimonies of many former activists concur on the point that military service presented an opportunity for anti-regime mobilization. Fernando Martinho, for example, the leader of the Coimbra crisis, went to the Mafra School and recounts that: 'It was 1970, there were people from the 1969 crisis, and there were clear signs of their passage [through the armed forces]' (Bebiano and Cruzeiro 2006: 90).

The Selective Opening of the Institutions

The replacement of the Minister of National Education, José Hermano Saraiva, arrived at the end of 1969, in charge during the extremely critical two-year period of 1968–1970, with the ousting of the young physicist José Veiga Simão, advocator, as seen previously, of the reformist and liberalizing wing of the regime.[27] This tendency was confirmed in 1970 with the arrival of the new Rector of Coimbra University, Professor José Gouveia Monteiro, who, in his inaugural speech, predicted that the imminent reform could bring new life to the university, and that this was the only way to overcome the hatred brought about by the dissent.

Monteiro thought that it was necessary to 'allow this to be done',[28] that is, to allow the reins of change to be in the hands of its members. In this perspective, pointing an accusing finger at the impediments lodged against the appropriate channels of renovation, Monteiro was actually stating that the students had been the victims of an effective situation of backwardness and it was indeed necessary to hear their motivations, erroneously considered destructive. Foreseeing that the tensions that had deeply scarred the academy could be channelled to produce a space of collective work with a view to the preparation of the reform project, Monteiro stated: 'I consider that the university should be depoliticized, bilaterally. I do not consider that talking about politics should be forbidden in the university, on the contrary. Placing politics aside, the university must work relentlessly towards upward social mobility'.[29]

While this statement should be viewed with caution considering that it merely reflected one particular position within the New State – albeit very close to that of the contemporary Minister of Education – they were in fact surprising words for an authoritarian regime. Practically all the more moderate demands that had arisen from the movement were considered legitimate. At the same time, any reference to the more radical and specifically political demands was abandoned, as was any inference on possible activists of the protest or hypothetical subversive plans.

In his interpretation, the new rector attributed a completely different identity to the movement, cleansed of its most disturbing and anti-system members, thus constructing an actor with whom the institutions could interact. It was also, as will be shown, a position upheld, from some points of view, by the actual PIDE/DGS, which had always defended the urgent need to create consensus in the university through initiatives aimed at channelling its dissident energy in an institutional form.

In Coimbra, the process of opening and repression by the authorities, inaugurated with the crisis of 1969, managed to achieve some visible results, which in particular contributed to the demobilization of the massive student block that had protested during the month of April. In 1970, the academic environment appeared so pacified, in spite of some minorities that remained active, that a delegation – composed of the Rector, Gouveia Monteiro, various teachers and eight student leaders who were still suspended from the university – was finally received by the President of the Republic. The objective of the embassy was to 'request for understanding and benevolence concerning the serious episodes' that had occurred in the previous year, and the repeal of the adopted disciplinary proceedings. It was Alberto Martins himself, the leader of the 'act of irreverence' of 17 April 1969, who read the formal apology to the Head of State, the latter, however, declined any understanding. In spite of the attitude of President Tomás, the delegation achieved some results, because by the end of the month, the Minister of Education, Veiga Simão, announced a general amnesty for the students with suspended proceedings.

This action began to be contextualized within Coimbra University itself. The argument sustained by the students who were against the mission was based on the idea that an action of this type would have been harmful to their Lisbon colleagues, primarily because it 'led to a breach in student solidarity, creating a bridge of preferential treatment with the institutions'. In fact, while up to the last months of 1969, the student dissident environment of Lisbon and Coimbra still maintained important elements of continuity from the beginning of the 1970s onwards – although Lisbon had already shown a more transgressive repertoire since the final months of 1968 – the paths taken in the two cities followed increasingly divergent directions.

The moderation of Coimbra was also criticized by radical publications such as *Cadernos de Circunstância* ('Circumstantial Notebooks'), which stated, with regard to the AAC's position on the reform of education: 'The dissemination of the education ideology as the great panacea is conducted in the name of the very academic associations that until very recently were presented as bastions of anti-fascism'.[30] The criticism also targeted the President of the AAC, Alberto Martins, who, during the strike against exams following the Coimbra crisis, had distributed a pamphlet on 'National education and economic development', which argued that the most important factor for economic growth was education. *Cadernos de Circunstância* responded to this position by accusing that 'what all these people criticize in Portuguese capitalism is its backwardness'.[31] The reformism of Alberto Martins' position is thus defined as 'a systematic attempt to recuperate and instrumentalize mass contentious initiative with a view to the redefinition of the system and its more rational reproduction'.[32]

This 'reformism' of Coimbra also raised different reactions in Lisbon's universities. By 30 April 1969 an Inter-Association Meeting had been held at the Faculty of Science of Lisbon. It had involved an intense debate between those who defended the need to lend unconditional support to Coimbra and those who refused any solidarity with their colleagues.[33] These cleavages would indicate, as noted by Marta Benamor Duarte (Benamor Duarte 1997), that the Lisbon students were apparently more acutely aware that the regime was undergoing change and that this change would also involve the university, but in a very different direction from that desired by the students. It was also evident that, under Marcelism, circumstances were altering and that, accordingly, so should the means of contestation be altered, which during the last years of the regime was becoming increasingly more similar to what was being carried out in democratic countries.

Following these lines, any and all negotiation with the institutions was rejected in Lisbon from 1969 onwards, and especially after the political elections of that year. The more radical students also abandoned any hope of using the legitimate channels of participation, a strategy that only continued to be defended by the PCP, which, as in the early 1960s, held strong to its belief in the need for double action, legal and illegal, without interference between the two and with the illegal sphere being as dissimulated as possible.

In Lisbon, the line of the organizations of the radical left would prevail, where there was no distinction between the two spheres of action, as the intensification of explicitly transgressive conflictual actions conducted by students demonstrated. Benamor Duarte also shows that in Coimbra, on the other hand, the rearguard of the academic struggle was primarily assured by communist members, and it is also here that a plausible explanation may be found for the different form of action with respect to Lisbon. While it had been Cunhal himself, back in 1961, who had criticized the so-called 'right-wing deviation' of the preceding years, by the early 1970s he felt compelled to denounce the activism of the radical left, in *O radicalismo pequeno-burguês de fachada socialista* (1970), due to lack of organizational-strategic capacity and poor theoretical preparation. In the path of Lenin, left-wing communism, according to Cunhal, was therefore not only ineffective from the point of view of the revolution, but also counterproductive and played, consciously or not, according to the rules of the game of fascism.

To summarize, the reciprocal accusation, between the old and new left, was that their action favoured the interests of the bourgeoisie and the regime, to the detriment of the 'real revolution'. *Rádio Portugal Livre* (Free Portugal Radio), linked to the PCP, in 1970 also took on the role of reprimanding the 'left-wing deviations' that threatened the unity of the student and youth movement. The young working class was considered, by this radio broadcaster, the principal combat force of the Democratic Movement which should also be used to reinforce the student movement. However, it was also stressed that the effectiveness of this young working class was threatened by various factors, such as the 'directionless, divisionary and paralysing action of pseudo-revolutionary students'.[34] The positions of the radical students, especially those of Lisbon, are defined by *Rádio Portugal Livre* as:

> [o]pportunist, which seriously hinder the development of the student fight, through left-wing verbalizations, that conceal positions of the most complete right-wing opportunism, fight against the work organized by specific objectives, push the associative movement towards anarchist discussion … taking advantage of this, Caetano's government presents the concessions that are imposed by the student fight as acts of clemency and generosity. Taking advantage of the verbalism of the others, it seeks to disguise the fascist reform of education as democratic and lead the students astray.[35]

In spite of these underlying conditions in Coimbra, characterized by a more moderate conflictual environment, more open to institutional dialogue than in Lisbon, a growing radicalization emerged in Coimbra towards the final phases of the crisis. However, the particularity of Coimbra was one of cohabitation and collaboration, albeit not always peaceful, between the new and the old left. The two political trends were represented, from the early 1970s onwards, by the Comissão Pró Reabertura da AAC (Commission for the Reopening of the Academic Association of Coimbra, CPRAAC), closely linked to the PCP, and the Comité Revolucionário dos Estudantes Comunistas (Revolutionary Committee of Communist Students, CREC), of Maoist leanings and linked to other groups of this tendency such as the Núcleos Sindicais (Syndicate Centres) and the Organização Comunista Marxista–Leninista Portuguesa (Portuguese Marxist–Leninist Communist Organization, OCMLP) (Cardina 2011: 144–45). In other words, with a considerable difference in relation to Lisbon, competitive lists would never be composed in Coimbra, representative of the old and new left to steer the AAC, but rather, the two alignments would continue to act within the same academic organizations.

Vertical Dissemination

One of the most significant long-term effects of the Coimbra mobilization of 1969 and its consequences was a process that could be defined as the 'vertical dissemination' of the contestation to the regime which, based on the student environment, reached the teaching staff of the university. It was in 1973 that the growth in the number of higher education teachers displeased with the regime became increasingly evident. These dissident teachers, when not prevented from exercising their profession, were closely controlled by the police forces. This sign is indicative of the vertical dissemination of the unrest that had surrounded the student environment in the preceding years: in many cases the students had become assistant lecturers and, later, full teachers. In fact, this was a phenomenon that most probably also occurred in other contexts, and would have involved the majority of the professions, taking into account the different faculties that participated in the protest: Medicine, Law, Engineering, Economics, Management and Finance, Letters and Fine Arts.

The first signs of the phenomenon referred to above became visible through the student mobilization's contamination of the country's elite sector, which was now broader with the first results of the opening up of university education. Unfortunately, there is no available data relative to the political position, at this particular time, of other professional categories, nor is data available for the same category relative to other times, that could convey interesting comparisons. However, the considerations that may be inferred from the limited documentation that is available, specifically with respect to the teaching staff of the Faculty of Law of Coimbra, are revealing of a situation where the decline of the regime appeared evident, merely a year before its fall, in the key sectors for the training and reproduction of its consensus and actual legal self-legitimation. On the other hand, it should not be forgotten that the major political and legal innovations of Portuguese contemporary history had always emerged from the very corridors of Coimbra University. It must be emphasized that this was an institution in which the most conservative legal–political theorization had normally coagulated, such as the opposition against the progressivism of the First Republic, which was later institutionalized in the Salazarist dictatorship.

The PIDE/DGS report in question thus summarizes the composition of the teaching staff of the Faculty of Law of Coimbra in April 1973: '14 right-wing persons, 12 left-wing, 18 with no defined alignment, which include some that have been active in the academic lefts and who have not been noted as having been engaged in any political activities that might contribute to better classification'.[36] However, in the opinion of the PIDE/DGS, although the overall picture gave the idea of a certain balance in the political field, this was purely an illusion. In fact, those classified as left wing were active in their ideas, contacts and connivance with students: '[W]henever there is an opportunity [they] will find interested listeners and will do everything within their power to brainwash the young university group in the party political ideologies that they defend or excuse'.[37] Rather controversially, the PIDE/DGS report emphasized that 'the same cannot be said of those I have classified as right wing', hence: 'Perhaps this would explain the appearance, unsurprisingly to us, of recent Law graduates with a truly scintillating left-wing political preparation, who will provide continuity, in the actual sector where they will professionally exercise those very ideas that were so generously and patiently pumped into them'.[38]

Notes

1. The Aveiro Congress was the 3rd Congress of the Democratic Opposition that was held underground, in the city of Aveiro, between 4 and 8 April 1973.
2. Interview of Jorge Wemans in *Pública*, number 79, 1997.
3. Offprint of *Avante!*, number 586, December 1967.
4. Ibid.
5. Daniel Joaquim de Sousa Teixeira was a student linked to the Liga de União e Acção Revolucionária (Revolutionary Unity and Action League, LUAR) – an organization that will be further discussed in the next chapter – who, imprisoned for having participated in subversive action in Covilhã, died when he 22 years old in Caxias prison, after a night of agony caused by an asthma attack during which he received no assistance from the prison guards (cf. Nery 2008: 32; and Flunser Pimentel 2007a: 410).
6. This was the name given to the occupation, on 25 November 1920, of part of the university premises used for the meetings of a cultural body considered elitist (Clube dos Lentes), aimed at demanding better facilities.
7. Binómio, Boletim da Associação de Estudantes do Técnico de Lisboa. Arquivo de História Social do Instituto de Ciências Sociais da Universidade de Lisboa (Social History Archive of the Lisbon University Social Science Institute, AHS-ICS/UL), student movement fund, box 9, labels from FG0836-ME0737 to FG0839-ME0740.
8. Coimbra PIDE/DGS report, 7 September 1968, in IAN/TT-PIDE/DGS-SC-SR-3529/62-3362-Pt.147, folio 12.
9. It should be recalled that it was in this organization that Salazar had started his political career.
10. Coimbra PIDE/DGS report, 19 September 1968, in IAN-TT-PIDE/DGS-SC-SR-3529/62, folio 60.
11. This traditional university music group was one of the cultural bodies of the Academy of Coimbra. It had been founded in 1888, under the name of 'Estudantina Académica de Coimbra' and adopted its contemporary name of 'Tuna Académica' in 1898. This body has always been dedicated to publicizing Portuguese music through various musical groups, a music school, and a workshop for the construction and restoration of traditional Portuguese musical instruments.
12. The Academic Orfeon of Coimbra is one of the eight autonomous bodies of the Coimbra Academic Association, and, founded in 1880, is Portugal's oldest choir and one of the oldest in Europe.

13. Coimbra PIDE/DGS report, 11 October 1968, in IAN/TT-PIDE/DGS-SC-SR-3529/62-3362-Pt.148, Coimbra student movement, folio 338.

14. Cf. Pamphlet of the Council of Delegates of Law Faculty, 17 January 1969.

15. Coimbra PIDE/DGS report, 21 January 1969, in IAN/TT-PIDE/DGS-SC-SR-3529/62-Pt.148, folio 215.

16. Coimbra PIDE/DGS report, 25 January 1969, in IAN/TT-PIDE/DGS-SC-SR-3529/62-Pt.148, folio 213.

17. Coimbra PIDE/DGS report on strikes against the exams, 13 February 1969, in IAN/TT-PIDE/DGS-SC-SR-3529/62-Pt.148, folio 81.

18. For a more detailed description of these events and on their consequences in Coimbra's student mobilization, see Bebiano and Cruzeiro (2006) and Cardina (2008).

19. Coimbra PIDE/DGS report, 17 April 1969, IAN/TT-PIDE/DGS-SC-SR-3528/62-3362-Pt.149, folio 349.

20. ISCEF bulletin on the events of Coimbra.

21. Ibid.

22. See, among others, Caiado (1990), Garrido (1996) and Bebiano and Cruzeiro (2006).

23. *Voz da Liberdade* Radio bulletin, 12 August 1969, transcribed by the Eavesdropping Services of the Portuguese Legion, in IAN/TT-PIDE/DGS-SC-SR-3529/62-3364-Pt.152, Coimbra student movement, folio 97.

24. The decree was approved, by the initiative of the Presidency of the Council, the Ministry of Defence and the Ministry of the Interior, on 4 July 1969, and aimed to give 'new wording to number 1 of article 24 of Law 2135 that promulgates the Law of Military Service', which regulated the postponement of military service for reasons of education. The new rule submitted the postponement to the student's performance, so that only students with 'good school conduct' could benefit from it. See Decree-Law 49 099, Diário da República number 155, Series I, 4 July 1969.

25. Coimbra PIDE/DGS report, 20 January 1970, in IAN/TT-PIDE/DGS-SC-SR-3529/62-3364-pt.153, folio 222.

26. Coimbra PIDE/DGS report, 3 November 1969, in IAN/TT-PIDE/DGS-SC-SR-3529/62-3364-pt.153, folio 439.

27. It is interesting to observe that the periods of most intense student conflictual behaviour led to the replacement of the minister of national education on certain occasions. This was the case of Manuel Lopes de Almeida, in office merely for a year and a half (between 1961 and 1962) and the same time of the Minister Hermano Saraiva. This detail appears even more evident when we consider that the average time in office of the ministers of national education was, between the post-war period and 1974, around 4.3 years, with a minimum, excluding the cases of Lopes de Almeida and Saraiva, of 2.5 years and a maximum of 8.5 (in this last case, the ministry of Fernando Andrade Pires de Lima which lasted from 1947 until 1955). It should also be noted that during the period of 1956–1974, the minimum time of permanency in the Ministry of National Education, excluding the cases referred to above, was 4.5 years.

28. *Diário de Notícias*, 20 February 1970.

29. Ibid.

30. *Cadernos de Circunstância*, new series, number 7, March 1970, p. 47.
31. Ibid., p. 47.
32. Ibid., p.48.
33. Lisbon PIDE/DGS report, 30 April 1969, in IAN/TT-PIDE/DGS-SC-SR-3529/62-3362-Pt.149, folio 187.
34. Radio Portugal Livre Boletim, 17 December 1970, intercepted by the Eavesdropping Services of the Portuguese Legion, in IAN/TT-PIDE/DGS-SR-1/46, 2495, folio 13.
35. Ibid.
36. PIDE/DGS report on the political tendencies of the teaching staff of the Faculty of Law of Coimbra, 12 April 1973, in IAN-TT, PIDE/DGS-SC-SR-3529/62-Pt, folio 154.
37. Ibid.
38. Ibid.

Chapter 4

Protest Cycle or Permanent Conflict?

The New Objectives of the Student Movement

Students Hung between Electoral Mobilization and Disillusionment

In 1969 the Lisbon student movement, although it had shown some renovation of its repertoire in a more radical sense, was still divided by important legalist currents favourable to the use of legal channels of participation, such as the imminent legislative elections. Marcelism, although criticized as the 'new tyranny', had also brought in intense expectations of institutional change, primarily through the adopted measures curbing prior censorship, the return from exile of the Bishop of Porto and Mário Soares, the renovation of the National Union in a direction that appeared to be more liberal, and new syndicate legislation that exempted elected syndicate leaders from the need to obtain official ministerial approval.

These expectations were mainly channelled towards the electoral campaign for the political elections of 1969, the first after the withdrawal of Salazar. These were also the first elections where the opposition was presented divided into two lists, at least in Lisbon, Porto and Braga: the Comissão Eleitoral de Unidade Democrática (Electoral Democratic Unity Commission, CEUD), composed of the ASP, various Catholics and a few monarchists; and the CDE, which grouped together those close to the PCP. The period of the elections was from the very beginning one of intense mobilization by the PCP. The communist Radio Portugal Livre stated that a new stage of the fight on the electoral field was being experienced:

> Audaciously and vigorously slashing open new gashes in the fascist barrier, the forces of democracy can give their utmost in their fight in the electoral field. Rarely outside the actual electoral periods would the political fight have attained the plenitude and vitality that are currently being recorded ... Declaring its decision to fight for concessions in the electoral field, uniting around common principles to fight for democracy, starting the instruction of a unitary

movement based on participation in the electoral act, the democratic opposition has not only dealt a severe blow to the pretensions
of the fascist liberalizing demagogy, but is also creating the foundations for a powerful development of the Portuguese people's fight
for democracy.[1]

In the campaign of 1969, the PCP and its list also received the support
of students mobilized by the EDE. The EDE was created in the wake of the
first demonstration against the Vietnam War, held in February 1968, by
young former militants of the PCP, such as Fernando Rosas and Amedeu
Lopes Sabino, and others who were never linked to this party, such as
Arnaldo de Matos. This organization – which would provide the founding
members of the MRPP in 1970 – marked a kind of 'exterior frontier' relative
to the CDE, although its relations with the PCP were more distant, having,
for example, a different interpretation on the significance of Marcelism.

However, in spite of having embarked on a path in the direction of
progressive radicalization, the legalist theses continued to be considered
important by the militants of this formation of the new left, in open controversy with the contrary tendency that was already being felt in the university
environments: 'We should reject the current concept according to which
elections is equivalent to betrayal, a slogan empty of any political content
in the present situation and whose consequence is the abstention and par-
alysation of the fight, suitable only for utopian forms, which will ultimately
produce right-wing consequences. It is necessary to study the technical possibilities of the legal work permitted during the electoral period'.[2]

The EDE always had good results in terms of consensus, as demonstrated
by the fact that, in 1969, a list of this organization, headed by Arnaldo
Matos had won the elections for the Board of the Academic Association
of Law, defeating a PCP list. However, the legislative elections were a real
disillusionment to the opposition, primarily student, which was to have
considerable influence in the process of radicalization.

As noted by Jorge Costa, 'in addition to the innumerable violations of
electoral law, there was very limited voter registration and massive [levels
of] abstention (above 50% in Lisbon, 42% at a national level): 15% of
potential voters actually voted' and 'the weak results of the opposition (130
thousand votes) are not deceptive with respect to the failure of the intended
endorsement of the regime' (Costa 2002: 25). The disillusionment with the
Marcelist opening and success of the elections, which had been strong elements of the mobilization in 1969, laid the grounds for the radicalization of
some sectors of the EDE that merged into the MRPP. While it is true that
the contrast with the PCP had already contributed to the emergence of the

EDE, in fact, at the time of the elections of 1969, this breakaway did not appear so radical. In this perspective, the EDE provides a very clear example of the path of a part of the student left, who, after the electoral disillusionment, abandoned the institutional and legalist thesis and embarked on a more radical path, contributing to the birth of one of the most active Marxist–Leninist formations in the Lisbon scene of the last years of the regime and during the revolutionary process, the MRPP.

Hence, as has been seen in the case of the EDE, it was above all after the elections that the process of radicalization and politicization of the Lisbon movement intensified, very much earlier and with greater strength than in Coimbra. Preceding their colleagues in both Coimbra and Porto, the Lisbon students not only adopted a more daring repertoire of contestation, but also more radical themes, whether from the social point of view, such as the 'sexual revolution', or the political point of view, such as the fight against the bourgeois State, whether embodied by an authoritarian or a democratic regime. At that time it was becoming increasingly more evident, including to the government, that the reopening of the academic associations could represent a minor issue, even perhaps an issue easily resolved, and that would have channelled the student dissent inside more controllable bodies, representing a sort of dam holding back extremism. This was a fairly reasonable strategic calculation by the authorities, who understood that the existence of a legal channel of representation could be an effective form of 'anchoring down' radical tendencies that might otherwise become destructive.

However, this solution, which had already been aired in an article published by *Diário de Notícias* in December 1968, arrived outlandishly late in response to the demands that had been formulated a decade previously. As noted by Benamor Duarte (1997), the students had by this time left the university and, once enmeshed in society, had already adopted new forms of dissidence and new objectives, such as the end of the regime and the victory of the proletariat. Hence, having partially won the fight for associative freedom, for student representation and for freedom of expression within the university, part of the student movement was ready to put aside the corporate issues and aim higher. This would be the story of the student movement in the final years of the regime, when it became increasingly more political and more Lisbon-based.

The Students and Socio-political Change

At Portuguese universities the political moment was going through a phase of progressive complexity, which was intensified by the disillusionment caused by the elections of the autumn of 1969. According to the inform-ers of the PIDE/DGS, the following currents existed at the universities in 1970: the PCP, Marxist–Leninist groups, progressive Catholic groups and the movement of democratic opposition, which were a reflection of national political life. Both the PCP and the organizations of the new left, especially the Maoists, had attracted a large number of members in university, second-ary and middle education, hence their membership had swollen significantly, as reported by the PIDE/DGS: 'Recent investigations and imprisonments give us an alarming vision of the expansion of communism and affiliated-communism in this sector'.[3]

At this time, the students most linked to the PCP tried to take stock of the activities that had been developed and the 'objectives and limits of the student fight',[4] especially in relation to the issue of the reform that was being prepared by Veiga Simão. The problem consisted of what position the students should take with respect to the reform:

> What could the students gain in participating in the reform? At an authoritarian university with archaic structures, both in terms of size and form, with paternalist teachers and students who consume acritically, where the work is individualist, where the major fight of the students is in the field of pedagogy, where the student associa-tions have timidly rehearsed the first steps of moving towards the intended courses with an expansion of their base of support, their participation in the reform, apart from the elimination of the most backward sectors of the university, permits: elimination of certain forms of repression and consolidation of the current syndicate struc-tures; linkages of the syndicate structures to the student base and recognition; consolidation of the conquests of the student fight.[5]

This was a strategic line coherent with that developed in the student sector by the PCP, since the most radical groups were rejecting any possible chance of collaboration with the institutions. The use of the legal channels available for participation and unity was the cornerstone of this line. Hence, participation in the reform was considered an integral part of the goals of the student movement, which would be reflected in 'an increased awareness of the student masses' and would contribute to 'unveil the classist nature of education'.[6]

On the other hand, this participation would enable the possibility of introducing courses that would stimulate a 'critical vision of the evolution of society and mechanisms of production, analysing our position as men and as technicians'.[7] It was considered that the duty of education in the capitalist system was to train and qualify middle and senior staff for the dominant class and for its perpetuation, as well as convey an ideology underlying the economic and social system. This situation could only be changed when 'the workers possessed economic and political power'.[8] For the time being it proved necessary to conduct more participative classes, with debates and courses open to non-students, but it was evident that: 'The fight against [course] contents fell within the limits of the entire super-structural fight. The system would accept any ideology even if it would not be taken to its consequences. Only by linking the battlefront against the content of education with other fronts will the students be able to advance in their syndicate conduct'.[9]

Lastly, the fourth point concluded on the specificity of the fight of the working class, peasants and students. The limits of this last one referred to the fact that the students 'do not belong to the production system and are bourgeois and future middle and senior staff'.[10] Therefore, it was necessary to clearly define the limits of the student fight, in order to integrate it with the class struggle, where a priority issue was the fight against the classist content of education. However, 'the vision of the students would always bear a bourgeois mark, [and] therefore it was necessary to educate them politically'.[11] The PCP's position was embodied in the creation, in 1971, of the MDE, which openly competed with the groups of the new left.

The MDE was also established after the elections, which were considered 'a springboard, based on the strictly narrow legality that fascism was forced to concede'.[12] The underlying rationale of the creation of the MDE was identified in the existence of 'a vast series of mobilizing problems',[13] capable of playing a unifying role in the action of students of various ideologies. The founding document of the MDE stated that it was opportune to create two different and complementary organizations, one for legal work and the other for illegal work: '[T]he inability to create two different associations would be political incapacity; using what has already been created, masking this action with pseudo-revolutionary language, is right-wing revisionism'.[14]

Moreover, it was important that the MDE should emerge from the bottom up, involving many political and ideological concepts and positions, as well as a variety of suggestions. In order to assure the maximum participation of all, 'the majority should always be considered and not the minority, dirigisme is denied, even though a decision centre must exist'.[15] However, the free manifestation of all political positions did not mean that plans should be confused, or that issues would be addressed publicly that could only be debated in the illegal sphere, 'unless one wished to offer a plate of easy arrests to the PIDE/DGS'.

Furthermore, it was opportune to make the most of all internal events of the school 'that emerge, as well as all phenomena able to boost mobilization, and the commemorative dates of important events should always be made the most of'.[16] Due to its ambiguity, the issue of legality required some explanation and so the document of the MDE specified that 'legal' was not considered to be that which was 'legal for fascism', and that 'legality is conquered through the action developed in the light of the day'.[17]

The Students and the Class Struggle

In fact, all the left-wing organizations considered the student sector as a strategic sector, even if they differed with respect to its role in the class struggle. As has been seen, the position of the PCP was that the students could never be leaders of the revolution, due to being inevitably linked to the bourgeoisie, and that the student fight and the fight in the factories should remain apart. In turn, the MRPP considered the students as the true revolutionary vanguard, which had mobilized and indicated the path to the proletariat. Albeit with diverse leanings, the different Marxist–Leninist groups were generally closer to the MRPP's position. The newspaper *O Comunista* for example, created in 1968 by militants coming from the CMLP, had, since its very first editions in June 1969, defended the key role of the students in their connection with the workers in its analysis of the major social fights that had taken place during that year in the factories and universities.[18]

The news bulletin praised the level of student mobilization achieved in Lisbon by December 1968, which had forced the government to shut down various universities, and reported the episodes that occurred in Coimbra during April 1969: '[T]he student fight was going beyond the corporate limitation, beyond the reforms of education, and into the field of attacking the bourgeois dictatorship (or even democracy)'.[19] Therefore, this very first edition discussed the role of the student in the revolutionary struggle and the issue of its relationship 'with the Portuguese people', primarily with the workers and peasants. In this regard, criticism was levied at the position of the reformists (i.e. the PCP) who still viewed the student 'as a privileged social category, alienated to the needs and aspirations of Portuguese workers'.[20]

In the opinion of *O Comunista*, in contrast, 'in spite of their bourgeois class roots, there is no doubt that the Portuguese student, and likewise the student mass of all countries, can be mobilized for the battle against the national bourgeoisie', and it was the duty of revolutionary organizations to 'be responsible for making the most of this force and ensuring that it escaped from the influence of bourgeois ideology'.[21] Apart from which, it was considered that the actual government's strategy sought to keep the student fight isolated from other social layers, through the process that I have defined as selective opening.

So as not to play to the government's rules, the student should therefore join forces with the oppressed, a union that could only be ensured through political militancy – in other words, through the implementation of specific tasks, for example: the ideological and practical opposition to the Colonial War; the propaganda of the workers' struggle; the organization of subscriptions to assist worker and peasant struggles; the holding of demonstrations in support of workers; and the organization of joint worker–student contentious activity.

All this work had a further important significance: to 'cure the student movement of its eternal opportunist, careerist and reformist diseases'.[22] Theories were also constructed around the need for defence groups with internal instructions, since it was considered that it would be 'impossible to evolve towards open and determined street rioting unless the demonstrators were structured and protected'. Hence, for the urban fight, militants should know how to defend themselves from 'police dogs, tear gas, grenades [and] truncheons, and should know how to attack and retreat when facing specifically trained riot police'.

In another edition, by this time in 1971, *O Comunista* thus argued that 'students can only prove their class solidarity when they are capable of mobilizing political strikes inside factories, provided that this activity is not used to gain personal power among the masses'.[23] The whole point of the student fight was therefore to contribute to the development of class awareness among the proletariat, 'towards making all workers aware of the daily repression exerted by their employers, in other words the way that the capitalist system is developed by squeezing the workers as much as possible'.[24] Hence, the students' role was to make the proletariat understand this situation, whose only solution was 'revolutionary fight, destruction of the status of employers, Marxist–Leninist revolution'.[25]

It is interesting to observe that all reference to the type of regime enforced in Portugal has disappeared. The fight was no longer against fascism, but rather against the bourgeois state and capitalism itself. What was intended was not the introduction of new rights or an opening of the political system through the establishment of equally bourgeois democratic institutions: '[O]nce organized we shall not require the bourgeoisie to grant us rights, because we will have the strength to violently grasp it from them'.[26] Thus, the ultimate goal was the affirmation of socialism, along the path that could be understood by 'reading Marx, Engels, Lenin, Stalin and Mao'.[27]

The University of Lisbon: 'An Authentic Boiler of Revolutionaries'

Resources and Repertoire of the Protest in the Stirring Dawn of the 1970s

In early 1970, one of the academic places considered most sensitive and crucial by the authorities was the ISCEF, in Lisbon, where a series of meetings were held, starting in February; among those who attended were twenty-one assistant lecturers. The most debated topics included the reform of education, the situation of the student fight, and the strategic line to be adopted in the future.

These first meetings, attended by some of the teaching staff, addressing the situation of the student movement and the decisions to be taken in the event of a harsh crackdown by the authorities, decisions that went towards an actual occupation, opened the path to the season of free courses. This was a new element in the repertoire of student conflictual activity that was simultaneously aimed at unifying, informing and politicizing the students. The free courses, held within the actual universities and in some cases by a few teachers, addressed various subjects, depending on the faculty that organized them. The first of these courses were conducted at ISCEF and were dedicated to the study of Portuguese capitalism. According to some sources, the free courses represented a decisive moment in the recrudescence of the student movement at the beginning of the 1970s:

> These initiatives came either from the student associations, in this case the AEISCEF,[28] or groups of students with strong political motivation, and aimed to combat the traditional hegemony of the PCP in the student environments. Publishing texts and documents on current affairs, translated from foreign Marxist publications, they provided many students with updated access to political debates that were taking place outside Portugal and which the censorship prevented knowing about. On the other hand, by confronting the teachers with alternative 'courses', they accelerated the political radicalization of the students, accentuating the failings of pedagogic education and the denouncement of the political commitments of the teaching staff.[29]

Support text number 1, drawn up by members of the AEISCEF, for example states that:

> This is not a question of 'physically' replacing the teachers by others who are more technically competent, more pedagogically 'wise',

more or less authoritarian; what this involves AND THIS IS WHERE
ALL THE IMPORTANCE OF THE FREE COURSE RESIDES, is the launch-
ing of embryonic basic discussions where, and through which,
people feel 'their' alternative, enabling working parties to test their
strengths in the context of a critical investigation of social phenomena, interspersing interventions in the course by groups that have
more diligently studied certain aspects of the matter, with the free
course thus being a truly collective and enterprising experience.[30]

The informer Glória e Vera Cruz, who from the late 1960s was the man
of the PIDE/DGS at ISCEF, noted that, during the free courses at this
institute, a news bulletin called 'Contra a Fábrica' was distributed which,
among others, reproduced a text by Simone Weil that had been extracted
from 'La condition ouvrière'. At the ISCEF there was an almost total stop-
page of theoretical classes which were substituted by free courses between
3 and 28 February 1970, and this situation was repeated during March.
These seminars therefore fulfilled the demands that had been expressed since
the mid-1960s, in some sectors of the student movement and among the
intellectuals of the new left, to seek new paths beyond those of orthodox
Marxism, as was also stressed by the authors of Cadernos de Circunstância:

> One of the fundamental theoretical tasks will be to gather and
> coherently articulate the elements of analysis and reflections already
> provided by all the left-wing communism, which goes from Sparta-
> cist ideology (Rosa Luxemburg, Karl Liebknecht, Franz Mehring)
> to the left-wing oppositions within the actual Bolshevik party (left-
> wing communists, democratic centralists, workers' opposition, etc.),
> including the theoretical ones of the Workers' Councils (Gorter,
> Pannekoek, Otto Ruhle, Mattick, etc.), to arrive today at the cur-
> rent representatives of the radical critique of State bureaucracy
> inside the countries of Eastern Europe.[31]

Some colloquiums held in the context of ISCEF's free courses were also
attended by members of the group formed around the magazine O Tempo
o Modo, one of whom is particularly recalled by the informer Vera Cruz for
delivering a speech titled 'Colonialist or colonized Portugal?'. Other free
courses were held on 'Economic systems and taxation in capitalism and
socialism: Comparison with the Portuguese case'.[32] One of the declared
objectives of ministering the free courses – apart from informing and providing critical instruments of heterodox socio-economic analysis in contrast
to those taught at the university, and in fact also in contrast to the interpre-

tations of the PCP – was to attempt to maintain the vitality of the student mobilization after the military conscription of the main academic leaders.

In the students' opinion, the government would thus leave the leaders alone, a plan that the informer Vera Cruz considered 'very theoretical and impractical', especially because 'however intense the action of the associative leaders, they could never reach through to the students except in rare cases', hence 'they will never achieve their intended widespread and deep awareness-raising'.[33] It was also evident that by 1969 three groups had emerged in particular: the first and largest was formed by students 'enthusiastic about school life', who joined in a provisional form and were unaware of the movement, the second was composed of very active students, and the third of 'those outside the movement but discontent'.[34]

The fact that the authorities considered these initiatives dangerous was confirmed by the constant presence of informers in the sessions, who later reported everything that had been debated and the appraisal that the different subjects had received. The students were aware of this one-off control and in various cases this led to episodes of extreme tension.[35] For example, as the informer Vera Cruz reported, while the basic texts of the courses were being distributed, the student Almeida Fernandes accused an individual who was there of 'being a PIDE', and this person was ordered to get out, 'surrounded by five threatening people'.[36]

Also due to these initiatives, at ISCEF the process of politicization appeared to have greatly progressed by this time, as would emerge from the texts presented at a series of colloquiums on syndicalism, among which the police found the writings of Rosa Luxemburg and copies of *Quaderni Rossi*, a historic Italian magazine founded in 1961 by heterodox members of the PCI, which was extremely important in the emergence of Italian workerism.

As a result of this increasingly strong politicization, the ISCEF was shut down, a decision that led to the occupation of the institute by hundreds of students on 8 May, who held a general meeting; but it was broken up by the public security police and they were forced to continue at IST, also with the presence of students from other faculties.

The political analysis activity conducted by the students of the ISCEF included a document issued in October 1970 defining a 'proposed line of action for the Associative Movement' aimed at defending the student associations as the 'baseline for the organization of the student movement'.[37] With this document, the student associations were henceforth definitively and openly considered instruments of political fight and no longer merely means of representation and defence of student rights. The objectives of this political fight also appeared inserted in a radical and anti-authoritarian speech which not only criticized the form of the political regime, but also the socio-economic organization of capitalist society, that was readapting the university to the 'requirements of monopoly capital'. Under these conditions, the student movement, threatened as much as the worker movement, could contribute to the 'radicalization of the class struggle in Portugal',[38] through the following aspects:

> (1) combat against the classist content of education and against the process of domination of capital over all society; (2) combat against the forms of placement and selection of students, especially against the process of political selection carried out at the university under the ideological veil of competence and knowledge (exams and grades); (3) combat against authoritarianism, indissolubly linked to the capitalist, pedagogic, administrative and policed university; (4) combat against student passivity and division, a basic condition for the so-called process of learning of the capitalist division of labour … ensure the placing in practice of student decisions, whenever necessary, paralysing the institution's operation, occupying university time and space, thus conquering under student control so as to place it at the service of the popular struggles.[39]

The strategy to implement this plan was radically differentiated from the mobilization programmes defended by the PCP and that have been delineated in most points of the present study. At this time, the police and security forces already appeared to be more attentive in distinguishing between communists and other currents, especially the Maoist, and declared, at the beginning of 1971, that this last current seemed to be primarily at the ISCEF.[40] It was at this establishment that a large part of the student activity developed during January 1971, with various general meetings that were always broken up by the public security police. This fact convinced various student leaders that the meetings open to all students should be replaced by secret meetings of student association leaders.[41] The institutional reaction once again shifted towards isolating the most politicizing activists, the effect of which, as noted above, was an acceleration in the process of radicalization and polarization.

On the other hand, the police had already issued various notifications to the student associations of the IST, the Faculty of Science of Lisbon and the ISCEF, addressed to their leaders, as a consequence of the notice issued on the initiative of the Minister of Education that the associations could not continue to 'travel around beyond its purposes'.[42] However, it was evident that none of the student associations had complied with the provisions, thus necessarily implying, in the opinion of the PIDE/DGS, that a general meeting of the public security council should be held, in order to provide for the immediate shutting down of the respective premises, with seizure of all furniture and instruments.

Nevertheless, the student mobilization was increasingly more wide-spread, embodied in an ongoing scenario of conflict throughout Lisbon's universities, and increasingly also extended to other schools, during all the final years of the regime. In May 1971, the Association of Science Students – under the control of an administrative commission appointed by the government between 1965 and 1969 – was shut down and occupied by the police and security forces for an undefined period, with 700 kg of 'subversive' propaganda having been found at its headquarters. A few days later, the actual Faculty of Science was shut down, to be reopened only in mid-June for the exam time, but under attentive supervision of the academic authorities.

The Faculty of Law

The focus point of greatest political innovation, particularly at an ideological level, was most probably represented by the Faculty of Law of Lisbon University. The faculty inaugurated the beginning of 1970 with a strike, from 21 January onwards, primarily based on four demands: abolition of the system of truancy and attendance notes, reduction of the number of students per practical class, opening of the faculty in the evening for working students, and equal representation of students through the Associação de Estudantes da Faculdade de Direito de Lisboa (Student Association of the Faculty of Law of Lisbon, AEFDL) in the governing bodies of the university (Lourenço, Costa and Pena 2001: 163). The headquarters of the propaganda section of the AEFDL were raided at dawn on 18 February, and the following morning the striking students entered into collision with 'various individuals who, armed with sticks, tried to break up the organization of the strike' (ibid.: 164).

The faculty closed by decision of the school council, the student association was invaded by the police who seized a variety of documentation and who conducted numerous arrests between 20 and 21 February 1970. By March, the Faculty of Law was still closed, which was why 'no events worthy of mention have occurred on the university campus'.[43] This consideration, however, was true only with respect to the short term, since in the long term these closures would contribute to the spreading of the most active students and contact with their colleagues at other faculties, with the success of an almost unitary movement. In fact, during the period that the faculty was closed, the Law students held their meetings on the premises of the Faculty of Letters.

The strategy of shutting down the university, that is, of thoroughly wiping out the physical space in which the mobilization of student resources was activated, was taken as one of the most common responses by the institutions in the last years of the regime. The normal operation of the universities was thus fairly syncopated at the end of the New State. While, on the one hand, this situation might have had some result in terms of demobilizing the student mass, on the other hand it showed three serious side effects, also highlighted on various occasions by the PIDE/DGS.

In the first place, eliminating the central headquarters of the mobilization, which was actually a headquarters under legal and institutional terms and more controllable, could have the consequence, as indeed it did, of further radicalizing the movement, which would find less institutional and less controllable forms of channelling its energy outside the university, in underground circuits. In the second place, the closing of the university, affecting not only the 'subversive' students but the entire student population, including non-politicized students, could bring out a reaction among those who had proved indifferent to the other demands of the movement. Finally, in the third place, it was easy for students who could not access the premises of their own universities to use the facilities of other faculties to hold meetings, whether for purely social or political purposes. In both cases, this phenomenon could contribute to spreading the mobilization of one university to others. This possibility, soon to be understood by the authorities, led to the later adoption of various countermeasures, such as the forced requirement, upon entry into a faculty, to present a card demonstrating the bearer's effective enrolment in that institute. With the new year of 1972, the conflict in the Faculty of Law had become even more radical. During February, the students boycotted the classes of teachers who were against the student movement, and held noisy meetings. The board of the faculty then suspended four students who had chaired the course meetings.[44] In response, the student movement called a meeting and the director requested the intervention of the public security police. This led to the various disciplinary proceedings served on Maoist students Maria José Morgado, João Pedro Chagas, Galamba de Oliveira and Ribeiro dos Santos. But in spite of the repression, the strike of almost all course years continued.

Mobilizing against the War

One of the most important innovations of this period was certainly the fact that the Colonial War was finally becoming one of the key issues of the student unrest, after years of ambiguous and hesitant attitudes. The radical groups considered that the time was ripe for what *Cadernos de Circunstância* defined as 'massive desertion' as a 'radical way to refuse to be used as an agent of repression'.[45] Hence, notwithstanding the ideological differences, it was important to bear in mind that 'since the context of war is what has ultimately determined the Portuguese crisis ..., the fight against the war will ultimately constitute the unifying element of the currently dispersed contestation'.[46] It is highly likely that the definitive acquisition of an anti-war stance, and the open support of desertion and flight from military service are linked to the lesser influence of the PCP in the student environment and to the stronger presence of radical groups that, as has been seen, contested the orthodox communists due to their moderation and entryist tactics, which also applied to their position on the war.

These appeals to flight from conscription and the logistic support that the organizations of the extreme left were able to offer in this context were an important component of the growing numbers escaping from conscription in the early 1970s, reaching 20 per cent of those recruited. However, it should be taken into account, as will be discussed in greater detail in the following chapter, that this growth in insubordination was not only due to political reasons, but also, in many cases, economic. Thus, the flight from military conscription joined the flow of emigration, which also intensified and became younger towards the end of the regime (Pereira 2012).

In turn, as discussed above, the PCP had, since the important V Congress of 1957, at the same time as it identified the path towards the future in the peaceful solution of transition to socialism, stated the need for the independence of the colonies, which had up to then been considered subordinate to the end of the dictatorship in Portugal. As noted above, the positions of the V Congress were replaced by those of the VI Congress, held in 1965, under the new leadership of Cunhal and the adoption of a more radical project for the overthrow of the regime. However, it should be noted that, in spite of this new direction, which also led to the constitution of an armed organization, the Acção Revolucionária Armada (Armed Revolutionary Action, ARA), until the very end the PCP upheld the firm belief that it was necessary to continue to use all legal channels of participation, including the electoral channel, and that the frontal fight against the regime and against the Colonial War would only have given rise to further repression. At the same time, the party continued to encourage its young militants not to desert, so as to undermine the armed forces from within – which, to a certain extent, did indeed occur in 1974.

At a time when various more radical political groups were emerging, which strived to stir up the student environment, the issue of the fight against the Colonial War and against military service was becoming a dominant theme in the repertoire of the student mobilization, which created new bodies specifically designed to deal with this issue. One of these bodies, created by the MRPP, was the Movimento Popular Anti-Colonial (Popular Anti-Colonial Movement, MPAC), followed by the Comités de Luta Anti-Colonial (Anti-Colonial Fight Committees, CLAC). These CLAC, together with the Angola Committee, were identified by the PIDE/DGS in the early 1970s as the principal 'anti-patriotic' organizations that acted 'towards shaking the morale of the young of pre-military age and, while engaged in this mission, convincing them to desert or not to attend their respective conscription'.[47] It was also noted that this campaign was growing on a daily basis and that propaganda aimed at inciting young men to desert was increasingly found in the country's universities. Significantly, the same propaganda began to be spread among the conscripts of the Military Service Conscription.[48]

In early 1971, the Radio Voz da Liberdade also reported the opportunity to join bodies called CLAC, quite unrelated to those referred to above, attributing these entities the following organization and duties:

> CLAC should be created in schools, in factories, at all workplaces and in military headquarters. The creation of underground cells of a small number of members working in accordance with conspiratorial rules in strict secrecy, with firmness and audacity, is a condition for the continuity of the fight against the fascist dictatorship and against the Colonial War ... The solid underground cells that constitute true structures of initiative and coordination are a factor for the development of mass initiative ... the anti-colonialist fight in all its forms and specifically in the form of sabotage and attack of the Colonial War machinery is fair and patriotic. The Portuguese people will not be free while other peoples are oppressed.[49]

On the other hand, the resistance and opposition to the war was linked to the fight against the reform of education due to its introduction of the limited period of three years of permanency in the same course subject, which, if not respected, implied prohibition from re-enrolment in that subject course. This was of enormous relevance from the point of view of the acceleration of military conscription. The relationship between the reforms of the exam process and the military demands was recurrently highlighted by the students at this time, and in fact on reasonable grounds, considering that the Portuguese State was permanently short of intermediate staff in the army, which actually became quite extreme in the final years of the regime.

Alongside this, the denouncement of the war expenditure followed an argument that was easily consensual among citizens, especially in view of the build-up to the dramatic oil crisis of 1973. The denouncement of military expenditure was also placed in relation to the issue of university resources. What was particularly contested was that decisions concerning the university should always be placed in a perspective that was utterly alien to the true interest of the students of cultural and scientific growth, such as when the demands of education were subordinated to those of the war, and when they were designed solely in a context of capitalist development.

The Social is Political

The student revolt of the late 1960s and early 1970s was also character-ized, in all countries, by a desire to transgress social rules imposed by a society considered authoritarian and reactionary in all its aspects: political, family-related, educational, sexual and cultural. While up to this point most of the study has been dedicated to the political discourse, this is because, in Portugal, above all due to the authoritarian nature of the regime, this dimension was given much more weight in relation to others in the student demands. Indeed, this was also typical of the student and youth movements of other countries of southern Europe, such as Spain and Greece (Maravall 1978; Kornetis 2013), which also lived under authoritarian regimes. This was also the case in Italy, where it is undeniable that the specifically political dimension of the student fight was predominant, and perhaps more urgent, considering the practical limits of Italian democracy, in comparison to the revolt against society and traditions.

However, this does not mean that more social and cultural issues were not aired in the discourse of the movements of these countries. This is evi-dent when recalling one of the greatest scandals that Portuguese students were accused of upon the publication, in 1961 in the news bulletin of the Via Latina Academic Association of Coimbra, of the famous 'Letter to a Young Portuguese Woman'. Here, the author, a medical student, expressed his deeply disturbing concern in relation to the situation of his colleagues, who lived in a state of oppression and lack of freedom that was almost deterministic: 'We are young. My freedom is not the same as yours. A high and thick wall separates us, that neither you nor I have built. For us, boys, living on this side, where we have a social order that favours us in relation to you. For you, girls, on that side of this wall: the disturbing wall of shadows and mental repression. Of statism and immanence'.[50]

A rather similar event occurred in Italy, when the news bulletin *La Zanzara*, of the prestigious Parini High School of Milan, published a debate on the position of women in society, seeking to examine the problems of marriage, female work and sex. The year was 1966 and the article created a national scandal in which all the main political parties voiced their position, which, with few exceptions, accused the three authors, the students Marco De Poli, Claudia Beltramo Ceppi and Marco Sassano, of being offensive to sensitivity and moral custom. The three were accused of the crime of 'obscene press and corruption of minors' and interrogated by the police, who, under order of the judge that applied a rule of 1934, forced them to undress completely to check for the 'presence of physical and mental signs'.[51] Over four hundred journalists, many foreigners, attended the trial and, at the end, the three defendants were acquitted. The episode is recalled as one of the first actions of the budding student movement.

Both these cases were events that are a very far cry from the transgressions that would take place a few years later, but they were already indicative of two aspects. On the one hand, there was an emerging contestation by young people, and especially students, of the predominant social rules, particularly with respect to sexual relations. On the other hand, the blocks of law and order (primarily conservative, Catholic and right wing) experimented with the repertoire of accusations that would become frequent concerning the new movements, accused not only of wanting to subvert the established public order, but also of conducting all types of moral perversion. Political and moral arguments were intrinsically linked, and in order to discredit student activists and later political militants, the authorities used the most varied accusations of obscenity, sexual promiscuity, moral corruption and the like. The sexual argument was in fact the most recurrent, used especially against girls. Hence, the most politicized students were frequently stigmatized not only due to their militant activity, but also due to their lifestyle which was considered immoral. These prejudices against militants and the fact that women were dedicated to political activity was not only a weapon used by the institutions, but in many cases found new meaning inside the actual political organizations.

Specifically concerning the feminist cause, it is important to note that the first Portuguese feminist organization, the Movimento de Libertação das Mulheres (Women's Freedom Movement, MLM), was only created in April 1974. In her last book, *Que Força é Essa* (What Strength is This, 2008) – the title retreading the name of a famous piece of music by the singer and songwriter Sergio Godinho – the founder of the MLM, Madalena Barbosa, highlights the non-existence of feminist groups prior to 25 April 1974. This does not mean that there were no more or less isolated personalities or the odd structure aimed at the defence of women's rights, especially at a social level, but that there were no specific entities or groups motivated by the desire for a change of the cultural, private and intimate life of women. These instances, considered as yet another aspect of social and political change, were linked to the 'second wave' of feminism that would arise following the Long Sixties and to the emergence of post-materialist demands that accompanied the movements of this period.

It has been noted above that in countries where political demands represented an urgent priority, as was the case of the dictatorships of southern Europe, less energy was found for aspects of social and cultural change. This was certainly one of the reasons underlying the difficulties of affirmation of openly feminist groups during the New State. But this was not the only one. As expressed by Miguel Cardina, in an article significantly named 'Views on an Absence' ('Olhares sobre uma ausência'):

> From the start, it is necessary to take into account the regime's thorough ideological investment in the creation of organizations focused on identifying women with the duties of 'mother', 'wife' and 'homemaker'. This was the actual aim of the creation of regime organizations such as the Mocidade Portuguesa Feminina (Flunser Pimentel 2007a). Also added to this was a legal construction that defined women as [people] under guardianship, the cultural siege raised by the censorship and its extension to the most varied areas of the daily life of a conservative Catholic moral foundation. (Cardina 2009: 1)

With respect to its relationship with the student mobilization, Cardina notes that the feminist issue 'acquired an increasingly important role in student intervention during the New State without, however, having effectively unblocked the limits to the eruption of an explicitly feminist discourse' (ibid.: 2). This was also related to the fact that the female component in the university was very much smaller. Nevertheless, although this situation had changed by the early 1970s and women had become the majority of the university population in Lisbon and Coimbra, hence, the actual composition of the student movement had changed, the student fights of this time never hoisted the flag of female emancipation. This would be justified 'by the urgent nature of all the other causes that were sitting upstream: freedom of expression, of association, the autonomy of the university, the reform and democratization of education' (Cardina 2009: 5).

In spite of these constraints in terms of student demands, by the early 1970s in Portugal, youth behaviour also seemed to be profoundly transformed. This becomes evident, for example, with the holding of the first major international music festivals, with the participation of great icons of the time, which attracted thousands of young people. This was an enormous change for a traditionalist regime such as the New State, and even more so

in the behaviour of the participants, described by the informers of the PIDE/
DGS with their habitual precision, and possible exaggeration.

At one of these festivals, held on 7 and 8 August 1971 in Vilar de
Mouros, with the participation of Elton John, a situation is described with
disdain where 'many thousands of people slept right there, wrapped in blankets and in the highest promiscuity' and where 'among other cases, there
were children with glazed eyes indifferent to everything, groups of men
holding hands and dancing around in circles, a boy lying down with his
trousers pulled down showing his backside, a guy so drugged and with his
muscles seized up that he had to be carried in the arms [of others], sexual
relations between two couples, all under the same blankets in the best lit
zone, indecency of all kinds and people lying close together'.[52]

Reference was also made to 'many students from Coimbra and others
from Lisbon and Porto and there were shouts of "independent Angola"
during the concert by Manfred Mann (who is a declared communist)'.[53] A
final note remarked on the reaction of some people who 'revolted against the
long-haired individuals, with some even shouting "go to work!"'.[54]

Notes

1. Radio Portugal Livre Boletim, 16 July 1969, transcription of the Eavesdropping
   Services of the Portuguese Legion, in IAN/TT-PIDE/PIDE-SC-SR-3529/62-
   3622-Pt.146, folio 155.
2. EDE pamphlet seized by the PIDE/DGS, August 1969, in IAN/TT-PIDE/DGS-
   SC-SR-3529/62-3622-Pt.146, folio 91.
3. PIDE/DGS report, 10 August 1970, in IAN/TT-PIDE/DGS-SC-SR-3529/62-
   3370-Pt.167, folio 254.
4. 'Objectives and limits of the student fight', folio of communist students, May 1970,
   in IAN/TT-PIDE/DGS-SC-SR-3529/62-3370-Pt.167, folio 328.
5. 'Reform at the University: Some questions on the objectives and limits of the student fight', a document of the student movement, May 1970, in ibid.
6. Ibid.
7. Ibid.
8. Ibid.
9. Ibid.
10. Ibid.
11. Ibid.
12. Document of the MDE, January 1971, seized by the PIDE/DGS, in IAN/TT-
    PIDE/DGS-SC-SR-3529/62-3370-Pt.167, folio 160.
13. Ibid.
14. Ibid.
15. Ibid.
16. Ibid.
17. Ibid.

18. *O Comunista*, number 3, June 1969.
19. Ibid.
20. Ibid.
21. Ibid.
22. Ibid.
23. *O Comunista*, number 10, May 1971.
24. Ibid.
25. Ibid.
26. Ibid.
27. Ibid.
28. Associação dos Estudantes do Instituto Superior de Ciências Económicas e Finan-
    ceiras (Student Association of the Higher Institute of Economics and Management).
29. http://estudossobrecomunismo.weblog.with.pt/arquivo/016544.php
30. 'An explanation', Free Course of the TE – Supporting Text number 1, retrieved on
    5 May 2014 from http://estudossobrecomunismo.weblog.with.pt/arquivo/016544.
    php
31. *Cadernos de Circunstância*, new series, number 1, March 1969, p. 7.
32. Report of the PIDE/DGS informer Glória e Vera Cruz on the ISCEF, February
    1970, in IAN/TT-PIDE/DGS-SC-SR-3529/62-3373-Pt.212, folio 92.
33. Ibid., folio 123.
34. Ibid.
35. A similar situation was at the origin of the events leading to the death of the student
    Ribeiro dos Santos in 1972.
36. Report of the PIDE/DGS informer Glória e Vera Cruz on the ISCEF, February
    1970, in IAN/TT-PIDE/DGS-SC-SR-3529/62-3373-Pt.212, folio 67.
37. Report of the PIDE/DGS informer Glória e Vera Cruz on the ISCEF, October
    1970, in IAN/TT-PIDE/DGS-SC-SR-3529/62-3361, ISCEF, folio 160.
38. Ibid.
39. Ibid.
40. PIDE/DGS report on the ISCEF, 14 January 1971, in ibid., folio 99.
41. PIDE/DGS report on the ISCEF, 25 January 1971, in ibid., folio 93.
42. PIDE/DGS report on the ISCEF, 3 February 1971, in ibid., folio 78.
43. PIDE/DGS report on the FDUL, 14 March 1970, in IAN/TT-PIDE/DGS-SC-SR-
    3529/62-3622-Pt.166, folio 24.
44. PIDE/DGS report on the FCUL, 11 February 1972, in IAN/TT-PIDE/DGS-SC-
    SR-3529/62-3376-Pt.196, folio 81.
45. *Cadernos de Circunstância*, new series, number 1, March 1969, p. 54.
46. Ibid.
47. PIDE/DGS report on subversive organizations, 17 December 1970, in IAN-
    TT-PIDE-DGS-SC-CI(2)-14643-7722, folio 151.
48. Ibid.
49. Radio Portugal Livre Boletim, transcription of the Eavesdropping Services of the
    Portuguese Legion, 12 May 1971, in ibid., folio 132. The plan was not very differ-
    ent, at a strategic level, from that drawn up by the PCP at the time of the prolifera-
    tion of the Patriotic Councils.
50. *Via Latina*, number 130, 19 April 1961.

51. *La Stampa*, 5 April 1966, p. 5.
52. PIDE/DGS report on Vilar Formoso International Music Festival, 1 August 1970, in IAN/TT-PIDE/DGS-SC-CI(1)-1311, folio 1.
53. Ibid.
54. Ibid.

Chapter 5

The Demise of the New State

The End of the Regime: Mechanisms and Processes

The Pluralization of Political Forces

As already underlined, according to Sidney Tarrow, a protest cycle is 'a phase of heightened conflict and contention across the social system' involving, among others aspects, 'a rapid diffusion of collective action from a more mobilized to a less mobilized sector' (Tarrow 1998: 42). In Tarrow's view, protest cycles often occur when citizens feel that the authorities are vulnerable to social pressure and social demands intensify. Protest cycles feature the emergence of new groups and the mobilization of new actors, innovation in the repertoires of action, and the elaboration of new cognitive, cultural and ideological frames, among other elements.

The growing mobilization during the last years of the Portuguese New State had all the hallmarks of a protest cycle. It played an important role in creating the conditions – mobilizing networks, resources and repertories of action – for the development of the social movements of the turbulent transitional period of the PREC in 1974–1975. As seen above, the student movement became increasingly politicized and radicalized from the beginning of the 1970s onwards, particularly in 1973, with more references to the worker movement among students, as the most radical among them viewed the working class as a natural ally. This reflected the influence of the May 1968 movement in France, and the workerism that deeply marked the student movement in Italy. It also signalled the intensification of worker struggles in Portugal, which began in 1968 and continued throughout the last years of the regime, escalating dramatically in 1973.

Struggles intensified within other labour sectors as well. There were strikes by fishermen in Aveiro, Porto, Viana do Castelo and Matosinhos; mobilizations by service sector employees, particularly transport workers and teachers; and movements involving tertiary sector professionals, such as bank and insurance company employees. Throughout 1973, the bank employees' union held countless meetings in Lisbon, Porto and Coimbra, and demonstrations were staged involving hundreds of workers. Also significant was the violently repressed protest of July 1973 by the employees of the national airline, Transportes Aéreos Portugueses (Portuguese Air Transport, TAP). The radicalization of issues and protests strongly affected the workers' movement, which engaged in go-slows and even in boycotts to press for a minimum wage and equal pay rises for all.

The struggle of the workers was also promoted by the creation of the semi-clandestine Inter-union Meetings (*Reuniões Intersindicais*) in 1970, the seed of what was to be the Confederação Geral dos Trabalhadores Portugueses-Intersindical (Inter-Union General Confederation of Portuguese Workers, CGTP-IN). This new mobilizing organization played a key role in creating the conditions for permanent agitation during the final years of the New State and the revolutionary period that followed (Barreto: 1990). This pluralization of protest actors, that is typical of protest cycles, also reflected a process of social modernization.[1] Social unrest was facilitated by a period of economic growth, which led to full employment as early as 1968 (Barreto 2000) and increased the bargaining power of workers. Between 1960 and 1973, per capita income grew at an average of more than 6.5 per cent per year, and some years it exceeded 10 per cent. The sociologist António Barreto notes, this was the period of the greatest economic growth in Portuguese history (Barreto 2002). At the same time, the costs of mobilization fell considerably given the relative openness of the Caetano government.

Social tensions and radicalization heightened after 1973, when the favourable economic situation ended and the oil shock and galloping inflation aggravated the deteriorating economic context. The Colonial War only added fuel to this fire. The war had begun in 1961 and came to absorb nearly 25 per cent of the state budget and 140,000 troops by 1973.[2] The two- to four-year compulsory military service was a sword of Damocles hanging over all young men of all social classes. As Nancy Bermeo underlines, 'Portugal's colonial wars were long and costly. Their profound effects on the lives of ordinary people were of the greatest consequence. By the early 1970s, it was rare to find a Portuguese family who did not have someone fighting in Africa' (Bermeo 2007: 391).

Because of the war, the economic and human energies of the country were channelled into the armed forces with seriously detrimental effects on national development. In addition to an increase in the number of young people emigrating from Portugal (Pereira 2012), one of the main effects of the war was a constant labour shortage precisely at a time when the economy was expanding. The war became a major issue in contentious student politics, particularly from the late 1960s onwards, when the hegemony of the PCP faded and other new left groups, particularly Maoists, gained influence (the latter regarded the African liberation movements as key players in the anti-regime struggle). As underlined earlier, radical student groups in particular supported draft resistance and desertion, while the PCP encouraged its militants to join the armed forces, undertake military service, distribute propaganda, and foster boycotts from 'within'.

Decree-Law 49 099 of 1969 established new recruitment rules, which permitted the early drafting of student activists. Inevitably, the PCP's 'mole' strategy spread to students active in more radical groups. The new rules made deferment for study dependent on individual conduct, so that only well-behaved students might benefit. After recruitment, the actions of radical students differed from those of PCP activists, particularly in terms of encouraging and assisting desertions.

Growing draft resistance among Portuguese youths during the final years of the regime largely explains the waning influence of the PCP and the rising power of more radical groups. The draft resistance movement was supported mainly by student networks, which helped draft evaders and deserters to go into exile. According to data published in 1988 by the General Staff of the Army during the first year of the war in 1961, 11 per cent of the young men called up failed to report for duty. By 1962 the figure had gone up to 12.8 per cent, in 1963 to 15.6 per cent, in 1964 to 16.5 per cent, and between 1965 and 1968 to 19 per cent. The number stabilized at around 20 per cent between 1970 and 1974 (Estado-Maior do Exército 1988).

The demise of New State was also marked by a deepening division between the regime and traditionally moderate sectors such as the Catholics. One of the most symbolic events that signalled this growing distance and the difficulty that the regime encountered in its attempt to find strategies to pacify society and contain tensions occurred during 1972 and early 1973. After the promulgation of the World Day of Peace by Pope Paul VI, a group of Catholics met at Rato Chapel on 30 December 1972, stating their intention to go on hunger strike in protest against the Colonial War and regime violence. This initiative was led by a group connected to the Anti-Colonial Bulletin and by Catholic students, although it was also supported by more radical groups such as the Brigadas Revolucionárias (Revolutionary Brigades, BR),[3] which distributed pamphlets around the Lisbon to garner support for the hunger strike (Almeida 2008: 269).

The protest continued on Sunday 31 December, with around three hundred people supporting the hunger strikers. In the afternoon of that day, the police gathered around the chapel, with riot vans and dogs, after which public security police officers entered the building and ordered its evacuation. The demonstrators resisted, sixty people were arrested, and the leaders were imprisoned in Caxias jail. The police had intended to close the chapel, but midnight Mass was held anyway, leading to the incarceration of the Father Janela. He was taken to the headquarters of the PIDE/DGS, and was only released after the Cardinal Patriarch of Lisbon intervened on his behalf. The repression of the activists who had joined the demonstration continued in the months that followed. Many were fired from civil service jobs. As a result, the public image of the New State was tarnished, particularly after the Patriarch of Lisbon condemned the regime for the first time ever, deeming it unacceptable that 'police forces should intervene in the sacred place as they did' (Almeida 2008: 271).

As underlined, Catholic sectors had been distancing themselves from the regime since the end of the 1950s. The strong critical position adopted by the Bishop of Porto, who accused, in his famous 1958 letter to Salazar, the regime's policies of causing the 'undeserved poverty of our rural world' (Almeida 2008: 45), contributed to legitimize the formation of a Catholic opposition. When the bishop was exiled, this distancing increased, but the Marcelist opening, which led to the homecoming of the prelate, did not resolve the problem. The Second Vatican Council 1962–65, under the pontificates of John XXIII and Paul VI, had also accelerated the formation of the Catholic opposition. The council resonated among Catholics all over the world, causing a 'tidal wave of new theoretical and practical ideas about the internal life of the Catholic Church, relations between Catholics and society, and the new challenges facing the world in the 1960s' (Rosas 2008: VI).

Among the new ideas emerging from the council, the most important were surely ecumenism and the right to self-determination of peoples, both of which were sanctioned by the Pope Paul VI's visit to Bombay (Almeida 2008: 293). However, as João Miguel Almeida highlights, in Portugal these ideas acquired a national specificity, and became inimical to the dictatorial nature of the regime and, above all, to the continuation of the Colonial War, which contradicted the council's message of peace. The path towards the affirmation of a Catholic opposition was not linear, however. It can be divided into two phases, with the turning point occurring with the emergence of Marcelism:

> Marcelism brought with it the diversification and growing complexity of relations with the Catholic opposition: some were attracted by the hope of a peaceful transition to democracy involving the Liberal Wing, or of evolving towards a position of critical support; other Catholics militated in the opposition with non-Catholic socialists (the CEUD/ASP/PS), royalists (the CEM), communists (the CDE), or in extreme left organizations (the LUAR, the PRP/BR). (Almeida 2008: 20)[4]

Thus, political opposition forces became more complex. What is more, some of the key political organizations of the transition, institutional and otherwise, were born in this period. They gained shape and defined their arena for action through a political struggle against the regime and with each other. In 1973, Mário Soares established the Portuguese Socialist Party in Germany, although the socialists (including Soares himself) had been active before then. The Liberal Wing – a semi-legal opposition force (Fernandes 2006) – was brought into the fold of the regime party, the National Union, and gained parliamentary representation after the elections of 1969. The Liberal Wing joined the political leaders of what were to become the parties of the right and centre right established during the transition.[5]

The PCP, an essential institutional actor of the transition, had been active in the underground opposition from the early days of the dictatorship, as it was the only structured opposition force that survived throughout the dictatorship. By contrast, the main actors and organizations of the radical left only became active under Marcelism, although some militants had longer histories of activism, in some cases as members of the PCP. These, mainly Maoist, organizations not only opposed the authoritarian regime, but also fought the PCP (for being too moderate), and among themselves, which contributed to radicalization and to the exacerbation of political divisions.

The Third Congress of the Democratic Opposition was held in Aveiro in April 1973, gathering the majority of the opposition forces together. The socialists were the strongest force at the congress, which was dominated by the issue of the Colonial War. The former protagonists of the academic crisis of 1962 and founding member of the socialist MAR, José Medeira Ferreira, submitted a document to the Congress, 'Theses: On the Need for a Plan for the Nation', from Geneva. It had a powerful impact. In it, Medeiros Ferreira called for the development of links between the political opposition and dissident officers within the armed forces in order to try to bring down the regime. This text also played a determining role in the formulation of the programme of the soon-to-be-born MFA.

This brief account shows how the regime was losing control over a broad variety of social sectors, and how groups galvanizing the political opposition were multiplying. At the same time, despite mutually destructive conflicts, the opposition was united in its antagonism to the Colonial War, be it for economic, moral, religious, ideological or personal reasons. The opposition forces focused increasingly on the armed forces. There had been a deep malaise throughout the military hierarchy in 1958–1962, which had resulted in various attempts to end the regime and to avoid starting the war. By the beginning of the 1970s, it was the sector that posed the greatest threat to the regime. The wave of conscription of dissident students into the ranks

of the army, particularly from 1969 onwards, contributed to the politicization of some key military nerve centres, such as Mafra Infantry School.

The moral, economic, ideological and personal reasons to resist the draft
combined with intensified youth emigration, leading not only to labour
shortages but also to a growing shortage of officers in the Permanent Staff
of the army (Carrilho 1985; Medeiros Ferreira 1992) precisely when the war
effort was expanding. This led to the enactment of Decree-Law 353 73 in
1973 by Minister of Defence Sá Viana Rebelo, which allowed officers of the
special staff to join the permanent staff as long as they spent a year at the
Military Academy and trained for six months with their respective branch.[6]

The Minister of Defence made no attempt to disguise the dramatic situation of the army when he presented the new legislation: 'This measure aims
to increase rapidly the permanent staff, which is dangerously depleted'.[7] But
the law only served to accelerate the shift among the officers of the permanent
staff, who had already shown signs of disaffection and politicization. This law
therefore contributed to the emergence of the Captains' Movement, which
affirmed in its first statements that, 'putting ahead of us officers who joined
the staff much later disarticulates the hierarchy itself and endangers military
discipline'.[8] Gradually, to the initially professional complaints were added
political demands. This led to the creation of the MFA, as it became increasingly clear that the only solution to the problems of the army was to end the
war, and that this would only be possible if the regime were to be toppled.

As a result of the progressive politicization and in compliance with a
political programme based on the famous 'three Ds' – Democratize, Decolo-
nize and Develop – the MFA spearheaded an attempted coup with the uprising of the Fifth Cavalry Regime of Caldas da Rainha on 16 March 1974.
The regime repressed the uprising and student protest, and peace was apparently restored. But a month later, on 25 April 1974, the movement toppled
the regime with a peaceful coup that became a revolution because of the
immense wave of mobilizations that followed. This wave was 'unexpected'
according to various authors, but it is argued here that it was a continuation of the cycle of protest initiated at the end of the 1960s, which only
ended with the radical transformation of the political system and the end of
Portuguese colonialism. However, before this 'anomalous wave' exhausted
itself and helped to bring down the dictatorship, there were many other
developments.

The Radicalization of Student Politics

Among the main players engaged in social conflict at the end of the dictatorship, students deserve a special attention. Student-led agitation became

increasingly frequent and radical in the universities and, from the early 1970s onwards, in secondary schools as well. New left groups radicalized student protest, and by the end of regime the student environment had become a key breeding ground for opposition to the dictatorship. It is significant that student mobilization and radicalization affected many countries, European and otherwise, during this period. It is equally significant that the repertoires of action, ideologies and demands were similar, be it under the dictatorships of southern Europe and those beyond the Iron Curtain, or under democracies with varying political systems and social structures such as Italy and France. However, these student movements each had national specificities arising from different political and historical circumstances: in Portugal, the movement was shaped by the authoritarian regime and the Colonial War in particular.

As in other European countries, the Portuguese student milieu had undergone a process of intense politicization and radicalization, particularly as a result of the growing influence of new left and notably the Maoist groups. To this, one must add open opposition to the Colonial War, and the concomitant rise of draft resistance and desertions. One of the first signs of this opposition and resistance emerged in 1968 with the first demonstration in Portugal against the Vietnam War, which was symbolically close to the Portuguese wars in Africa. But the more visible effects of the radicalization of student demands and repertoires of action became clearer from the beginning 1970 onwards, particularly in 1972 when students began to act outside university campuses, and urban guerrilla actions and openly anti-capitalist demands became frequent.

One of the first student-led urban guerrilla actions took place on 16 May 1972, when the public security police dispersed a demonstration of seven hundred students who had gathered at the Faculty of Medicine in the Santa Maria Hospital. In the late afternoon of that day, around fifty students of the IST and the ISCEF gathered for another demonstration on Almirante Reis Avenue in Lisbon – a very busy avenue near the centre of town – where they proceeded to destroy the entrances of three banks. They were harshly repressed by the public security police, who arrested twenty youths, most of whom were students at the ISCEF or the IST, or from the Faculty of Medicine.[9]

From that time on, students acted outside the universities and attempted to establish lines of communication with the general population, trying to disseminate and justify their demands, the significance of which was minimized by the mainstream press. The key issues in most student communiqués were the denunciation of Portuguese policy in Africa (news of which was found in the international press) and of police repression of students.

The latter was the most frequently mentioned in student 'Communiqués to the Nation', 'to the Portuguese population' or 'to the country', not only because police repression in the universities was increasing but also because the issue commanded citizen sympathy and solidarity.

The denunciation of police violence against peaceful youths – including women – whose only crime was to call for a better level of education that would benefit the country, as most of their communiqués highlighted, had a significant impact on public opinion. As some PIDE/DGS reports warned, violent tactics should not be insisted upon, so as to avoid the creation of 'martyrs'. However, the university was heavily policed, and most Lisbon institutes were under nearly constant police surveillance and control.

As the academic year of 1971/72 ended, even exams were undertaken under police surveillance. The start of the new academic year in October 1972 brought no improvement; indeed, the conflict took a turn for the worse. On 12 October, a man suspected of being a PIDE/DGS informer was prevented from entering the ISCEF and surrounded by a large number of students until two agents of that police force arrived. The police were unable to recognize the person in question, and great confusion ensued. According to official sources, the officers felt threatened and shot 'into the air', injuring two students. One of them was a law student, José Ribeiro dos Santos, who had been known to the police since 1967 and was a militant of the MRPP. He did not survive his wounds and died in hospital.

A large demonstration was held during his funeral on 14 October, which led to more clashes with the police. After the ceremony was over, conflicts burst out in various parts of the city. Twenty people, among them sixteen students, were arrested by the PSP and handed over to the PIDE/DGS. According to official reports, they were arrested because they had been part of a group of around thirty youths who, armed with stones, had 'walked down the Calçada da Boa Hora[10] shouting "assassins, assassins"'.[11]

In the meantime, the PCP continued with its legal strategy. In 1973, it supported the creation of the Comissão dos Estudantes Democráticos de Lisboa (Lisbon Democratic Student Commission, CEDL) to unite 'all anti-fascist students pursuing democratic goals, within the possibilities open to the student associations'.[12] However, the initiative taken that year with the greatest visibility was led by radical new left, particularly Maoist, groups on the streets of Lisbon, who used more aggressive and direct methods of struggle.

In May 1973, less than a year before the coup of 25 April 1974, these transgressive protest methods intensified, as suggested by the very high number of imprisonments that month (65). It should be emphasized that students had begun to act beyond the boundaries of the universities years before, making increasing social, political as well as educational demands. They physically 'exited' educational 'sites' – the campus and university premises – and became increasingly active in other urban areas. Initially, this presence was felt mainly in city centres, particularly in Lisbon, but also in Coimbra and Porto. The latter two became critical arenas for demonstrations and confrontations with the police. Later, students began to act in the urban periphery, and came into contact with poor people.

The first student demonstrations in the urban periphery took place on 11 May 1973. The group of students from the Lisbon Law Faculty organized the first protest in the Boavista district in Lisbon together with the MRPP. Cars were placed in the middle of the streets to block traffic, and stones were hurled at the police station.[13] The demonstrators dispersed when the police arrived, but then carried on up Almirante Reis Avenue to Chile Square, where they shattered the windows of the Fonsecas & Burnay bank. The aim of the students was to denounce poor living conditions in Boavista; the protest was also a direct forerunner of one of the first and broadest movements of the revolutionary period, the house occupations movement. This began in Boavista a few days after the revolution, on 2 May 1974, when families from the Boavista shantytown occupied 270 unfinished council houses. Boavista had grown exponentially and in an uncontrolled way from the 1960s onwards as a result of a broad process of urban expansion following a wave of immigration to the cities from rural areas. This process was unplanned and unregulated, and the construction and distribution of social housing was slow and insufficient (Ramos Pinto 2013). At the end of 1973 and during the first months of 1974, student actions such as lightning demonstrations, meetings, protests and actions against banks were an almost daily occurrence. Students forged a repertoire of protest, increasingly outside university areas and on the streets of the city. This was the forerunner of the wave of urban mobilizations that characterized the years of the revolution.

Increased Repression

Significantly, the imprisonment of students increased notably during the last years of the regime, peaking in 1973. The graphs below on political and student imprisonments between 1956 and 1974 offer a more detailed picture.[14] The total number of imprisonments for the period was 7,339, of which 939 were students. This means that students represented nearly 13 per cent of all those imprisoned for political reasons between 1956 and 1974, an average of about 50 student imprisonments per year. Also significant, in just the first four months of 1974 (until 25 April) 43 students were imprisoned, more than double the annual average for the period as a whole. There are therefore two curves: one for non-students and another for students. The two curves coincide at many points and undergo a similar progression. The student curve peaked in 1973, when students accounted for nearly half of all those imprisoned and were the social group most affected by police repression. The decline in 1974 is deceptive, since it is only a result of the fact that the regime, and the PIDE/DGS, ceased to exist after 25 April.

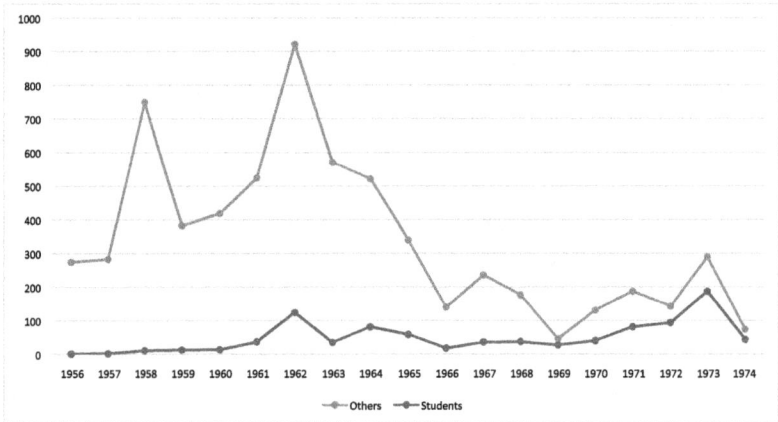

Figure 5.1. Imprisonment of students by the PIDE/DGS, 1956–1974 (Source: IAN/TT, PIDE/DGS Archive, Political Prisoners File)

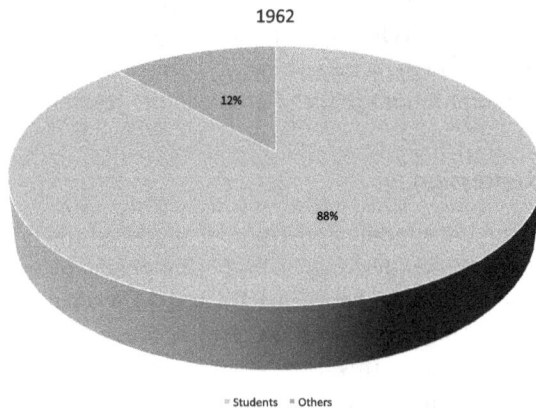

Figure 5.2. Political imprisonments in 1962 (Source: IAN/TT, PIDE/DGS Archive, Political Prisoners File)

1974

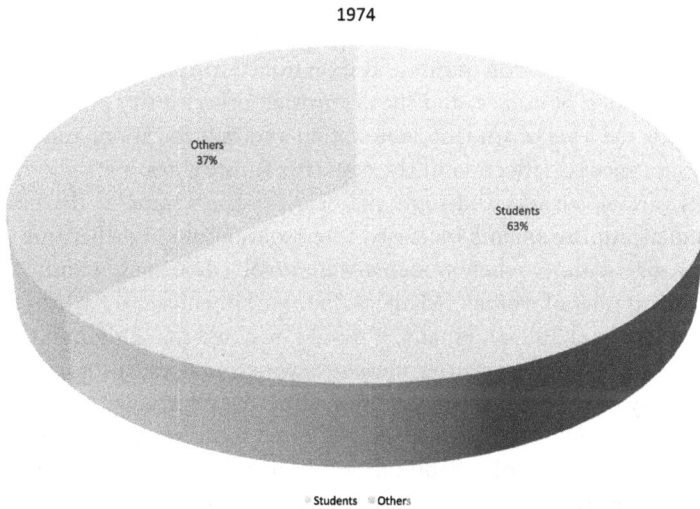

Figure 5.3. Political imprisonments in 1974 (Source: IAN/TT, PIDE/DGS Archive, Political Prisoners File)

In order to enable a better understanding of the increased percentage of student imprisonments in the total number, figures 5.2 and 5.3 show the proportion of student imprisonments in 1962 and 1974. In 1962, there were 1,045 political imprisonments, of which only 12 per cent (124) involved students. There was strong worker and student agitation in 1962, but the proportion of student imprisonments was lower than it was during the last years of the regime. In 1974, until 25 April, there were 117 political imprisonments, of which 43 (37 per cent) involved students. This is not a coincidence and is due to the short period under analysis (the figure for 1973 is similar: of a total of 476 political imprisonments, 39 per cent, 187, involved students). Figure 5.4 shows the percentage of non-student and student political imprisonments for the whole period.

It is clear that in the early 1970s, which were characterized by the radicalization of student protest, there was a notable increase in the participation of younger students, many still in secondary school. This is confirmed by the data on imprisoned students shown in Figures 5.5 and 5.6. In 1973, 24 per cent of students who were jailed were less than 19 years old; in 1962 there had only been 7 per cent in this age bracket.

As described above, most of these imprisonments happened over the course of increasingly frequent student demonstrations and university occupations. The rise in student political arrests was partly determined by changes in the repertoire of student protest, with the adoption of increasingly disruptive forms of protest, including lightning demonstrations, often involving the destruction of cars and shop fronts, irruptions in lecture halls, the interruption of classes, and the occupation of university premises. This highlights the level of student contestation and radicalization, and the dramatic process of disaffection of the country's future elites.

As various authors and some political prisoners state, as the number of student imprisonments increased interrogation methods became more violent, particularly when students were involved, among whom were a growing number of women (Madeira, Flunser Pimentel and Farinha 2007; Flunser Pimentel 2007a). Finally, it should be noted that although the government abolished the security measures, which prolonged imprisonment indefinitely beyond the terms established by the courts, with the reform of the Penal Code, trials increasingly referred to defendants as 'criminals with little likelihood of rehabilitation' or to the crime of terrorism. This meant that prison terms became much longer, and obviated the need for the security measures.

While 1973 was the year in which detention periods were shortest (it was also the year with the highest number of student arrests),[15] one of the longest prison sentences for political crimes, particularly for students, was issued that year. In February 1973, the last and most significant political cases were heard against students accused of military sabotage. The five students on trial all belonged to a Marxist–Leninist group associated with the newspaper *O Comunista*, were all between 23 and 26 years of age and,

1956–1974

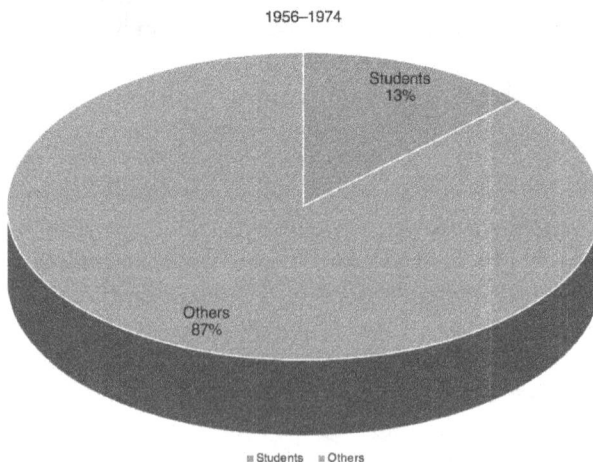

Figure 5.4. Political imprisonments between 1956 and 1974 (Source: IAN/TT, PIDE/DGS Archive, Political Prisoners File)

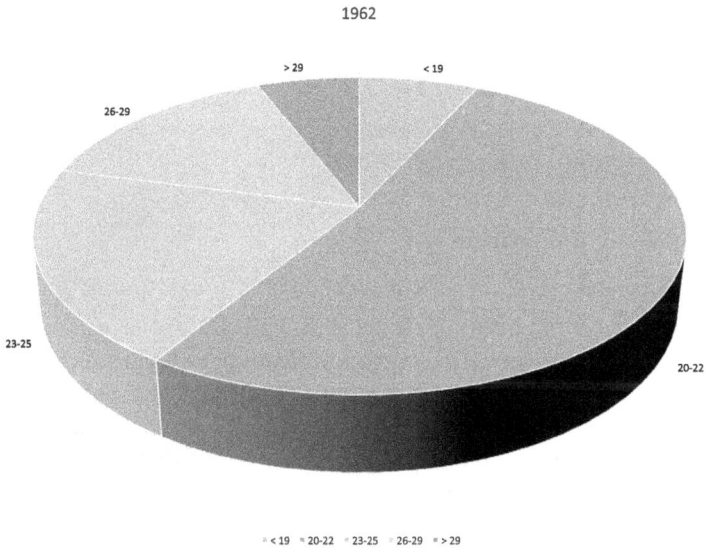

1962

Figure 5.5. Ages of students imprisoned in 1962 (Source: IAN/TT, PIDE/DGS Archive, Political Prisoners File)

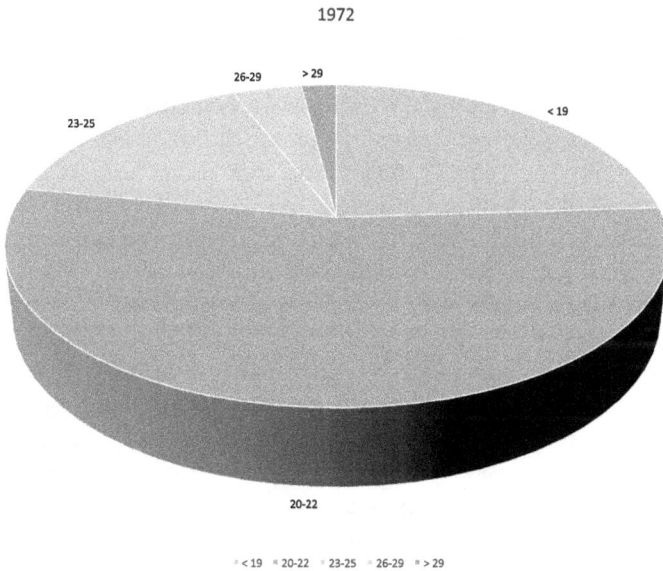

1972

Figure 5.6. Ages of students imprisoned in 1974 (Source: IAN/TT, PIDE/DGS Archive, Political Prisoners File)

as the prosecution pointed out, were all serving in the army. They were charged with encouraging desertion and their sentences were exemplary, ranging from eight to twelve years, which they had to serve under the same security measures applied to 'hardened criminals'.[16] This also shows that subversive actions by students serving in the armed forces continued until the overthrowing of the regime.

Left-Wing Competition

During the last two years of the regime, two processes that had begun in the 1950s came together and had a growing influence on radical groups within the student associations: the formation of a 'left' to the left of the PCP, and the politicization of the student milieu. The phase of conflict and competition on the left began, so that the pluralization initiated during the first protest cycle reached a new peak. This was marked by the Maoist schism and the abandonment of the unitary path of the PCP. The PCP lost its hegemony over the politics of opposition to the New State. This was the second great turning point in the twentieth-century history of conflictive politics in Portugal. It followed the phase initiated in the first years of the military dictatorship founded in 1926, when the PCP replaced the anarcho-syndicalists as the main point of reference of working-class militants, backed by the ideological and material support of the Soviet Union and the party's organizational culture, which prepared it for clandestine action (Palacios Cerezales 2011).

The communists and socialists, who had always presented joint electoral lists, had already split into two separate groups during 1969. As noted above, the communists and some Catholics came together in the CDE, while the socialists joined with some Catholics and royalists to form the CEUD in Lisbon, Porto and Braga, where they were unable to agree on joint communist–socialist lists. This was partly because the socialist group led by Mário Soares, which was to become the PS in 1973, had greater expectations regarding the Marcelist spring.

The universe of opposition forces had never been as fluid as it was at this point. Within the radical left even the smallest ideological differences led to splits or harsh criticism by rival groups, although everyone was equally critical of the reformist position of the PCP. Catholic groups were also involved. Some of the latter chose to support extreme left organizations such as LUAR and the Revolutionary Brigades, which opted for violent action (Almeida 2008).

Thus, the radicalization and pulverization of opposition forces were twin processes that marked conflictive politics during the last two years of the regime. They emerged alongside the two other aforementioned tendencies towards selective institutional opening and repression. The first phases in the process of fragmentation of the opposition at the end of the first protest cycle (1964–65) have already been described in previous chapters. The first Maoist schism that led to the establishment of the FAP/CMLP also came about during a period of strong repression of the PCP, which mutilated the working class and student sectors of the party. Political radicalization and competition on the left were frequent during this phase. Like successive Marxist–Leninist groups, the founders of the CMLP accused the PCP of giving up on revolutionary action in order to mobilize the electorate. Cunhal himself took that criticism on board when he reaffirmed the need for struggle against the 'right-wing deviation' of the preceding years at the 1965 party congress.

Indeed, because it was barred from any legal representation, the PCP could only undertake extra-institutional action and it was forced to compete with groups to the left to limit the breakdown of consensus among an increasingly radical opposition. The ARA, the communist armed action group, was established in this context of competition with more radical left groups. The ARA only carried out its first action in 1970 but it had been formed in 1966, after a trip to Moscow and Cuba by PCP leaders Raimundo Narciso and Rogério de Carvalho (Narciso 2000). Despite these efforts, the PCP was fated to lose ground to other extreme left organizations, particularly within the universities. This became particularly evident after the elections and academic crisis of 1969.

Despite the strategic shift imposed by Cunhal against the 'right-wing deviation', the PCP continued to focus mainly on electoral mobilization to take advantage of legal channels for political participation. Because of this, the party was increasingly accused of reformism or, in the new Marxist–Leninist terms coined during the Sino-Soviet conflict, of 'divisionism' and even 'treachery'.

Students and the Revolution

Extreme Left Trajectories in Portugal

The Maoist universe became increasingly complex from 1968 onwards,[17] when the few leaders of the CMLP who had not been jailed began to publish the news bulletin *O Comunista*. After a brief flirtation with Trotskyism, the group organizing this publication, which survived for fourteen issues, joined a group of activists who published *O Grito do Povo* (The Cry of the People) and were based in the north. The OCMLP was set up in 1972 as a result of these contacts, and from it was formed the União Comunista para a Reconstrução do Partido Marxista–Leninista (Communist Union for the Reconstruction of the Marxist–Leninist Party, UCRPML).

The Portuguese Partido Comunista de Portugal Marxista–Leninista (Marxist–Leninist Communist Party, PCP-ML) was another Maoist group that emerged from the fragmentation of the CMLP. It went on to publish *Unidade Popular* (Popular Unity). There were two other groups in the byzantine Maoist universe of the early 1970s that emerged from the CMLP and were set up by a group of militants responsible for *O Bolchevista* (The Bolshevist) magazine: the Comité de Apoio à Reorganização do Partido Marxista–Leninista (Committee to Support the Reorganization of the Marxist–Leninist Party, CARPML) and the União Revolucionária Marxista–Leninista (Marxist–Leninist Revolutionary Union, UR-ML).

The MRPP was the only Maoist organization that did not emerge from the CMLP, although also having some roots in the PCP. It was closely connected with the university, and established on 18 September 1970 by militants who had gained experience in the Student Democratic Left. The creation of the MRPP made the split with the PCP irreparable, and it led to the definitive abandonment of any attempt to take advantage of legal channels for political participation. The institutional and electoral attitude of the PCP was even seen as a form of collusion with the regime. Some of the main student leaders of the 1960s and 1970s, such as Fernando Rosas and Saldanha Sanches who had already suffered from violent repression, were MRPP militants. The MRPP was divided into two sections, the Federação dos Estudantes Marxistas–Leninistas (Federation of Marxist–Leninist Students, FEML) to mobilize students, and the MPAC for the anti-colonial struggle.

Another group led to the publication of *Cadernos de Circunstância*, launched in Paris in 1967 by intellectuals who had gone into exile in France to escape the 1963–65 wave of imprisonments. Some, like Manuel Villaverde Cabral, had participated in the founding of the CMLP with Francisco Martins Rodrigues; others, like João Freire and José Maria Carvalho Ferreira, had ties with anarchism and workerism, respectively. The *Cadernos*, which was published until 1970, was hard to classify in the Portuguese left-wing communism, and was closer to Italian workerism and to the writings of authors such as Mário Tronti and António Negri, with whom the editors had contact.

Finally, among the truly revolutionary organizations connected with the new left and having origins in the student movement, there was the FPLN. From it emerged the BR in 1971, and the PRP/BR in 1972, the latter headed by Carlos Antunes and Isabel do Carmo. The BR maintained more or less peaceful links with the FPLN working from the headquarters of the Radio Voz da Liberdade in Algiers. By contrast, while some members of the PRP were initially welcomed by the FPLN, later there was a dramatic schism within this formation.

This schism was not only personal, but also a result of different views on how to combat Salazarism and oppose the Colonial War. It was further complicated by the Chilean coup of 11 September 1973, an event that had a major impact on different currents and positions. Different groups had dramatically different readings of this event, but they always reflected internal group struggles, and their basic ideological premises. Thus, the FPLN (as well as the PCP) believed that anti-fascist unity was the only way to avoid a repetition of the Chilean episode, with the more radical elements considering such a 'social democratic' strategy as the cause of the coup in Chile. This argument was explicitly deployed as a justification for the PRP split from the FPLN:

> The revisionists and social democrats want bourgeois alternatives, but the recent Chilean example shows how this can destroy the pacifist and legalist path, which always leads to adventurism. The only solution is a socialist revolution with the takeover of power by the proletariat. But this is only possible through organized revolutionary action. Only the revolutionary violence of the workers can oppose the violence of the bourgeoisie. At this time, the internationalist nature of the revolution is amplified by joining the working class struggle with the struggle for liberation.[18]

It is worth underlining that all this had a direct impact within the universities, since students were protagonists in this competition between groups – the working class tending to remain faithful to the PCP.

This competition was frequently explained in the publications, radio programmes and informational materials of these organizations, which denounced each other with increasing vehemence, offering details and specifics about competing groups. The PIDE/DGS easily intercepted and used this information, particularly the details broadcast by the Radio Voz da Liberdade and Radio Portugal Livre, which offered valuable information about the opposition milieu and were tapped by the Portuguese Legion.

Marxism–Leninism among Students

Maoism was the 'Marxist heresy' that dominated the university and Portuguese opposition in general, mainly because of the colonial issue and its strong third-world component. The União dos Estudantes Comunistas Marxistas–Leninistas (Union of Marxist–Leninist Communist Students, UEC-ML) also participated in the V Congress, during which the first Marxist–Leninist organization in Portugal, the CMLP, became the PCP-ML. The UEC-ML became the youth organization of the PCP-ML, and its information organ was *Servir o Povo* (Serve the People). The historian Jorge Costa notes that the position of the EUC-ML as expressed by Serve the People was that militants should listen to 'the radios of Peking and Tirana' and establish strong links with the proletariat (Costa 2002: 26 and 31).

The IST-based Comités Comunistas Revolucionários Marxistas–Leninistas (Marxist–Leninist Revolutionary Communist Committees, CCRML) had a significant influence among the Maoist groups. As in Coimbra, another organization that was active among students was, as underlined, the CREC. It was linked to the Núcleos Sindicais and the OCMLP, but its ideology was quite unclear, making it difficult to ascertain the dominant current within the group. In addition to opposing the Colonial War and supporting the Movimento Popular de Libertação da Angola (Angolan Popular Liberation Movement, MPLA), it evinced somewhat 'anarchic' tendencies as expressed in their slogans 'Long Live Libertarian Socialism' and 'Long Live Libertarian Communism'.[19] The CREC was also open to militants of a variety of tendencies, such as the historical leader of the PCP who was held in Peniche prison, Dias Lourenço, and Palma Inácio, the leader of LUAR. The CREC also established the Serve the People committees[20] and published *Viva a Revolução* (Long Live the Revolution).

As seen before, the MRPP was one of the first and most important Marxist–Leninist organizations established by student initiative at the end of the 1960s. Its foundation signalled the final break of many radical students with the PCP (some of whom were the founders of the EDE). This break came in the wake of the electoral mobilization of October 1969, partly because of disillusionment with the Marcelist Spring, which led to a process of gradual radicalization. The MRPP and its various sections, the FEML and CLAC, were the organizations that were most frequently mentioned in police files on subversive groups in the universities.

The MRPP published its theoretical bulletin *Bandeira Vermelha* (Red Flag) as of its foundation, and from 1971 onwards published *Luta Popular* (Popular Struggle), its dissemination bulletin. Its student organization, the FEML, published the information bulletin *Guarda Vermelha* (Red Guard). From the outset, the MRPP claimed that the PCP had adopted a revisionist ideology and had therefore ceased to represent the proletariat and become a 'social-fascist' party. The PCP was as much of an enemy as the regime itself; it was an accomplice to the regime because of its long-standing legalist and electoralist position, which – MRPP militants thought – helped to legitimize the New State.

Two other points distanced the MRPP from the PCP. Firstly, like other organizations born out of the student movement, the MRPP espoused the belief that students had a vanguard role to play in the revolutionary struggle, while the PCP believed they played second fiddle to the proletariat. Secondly, like the rest of the radical left, it was believed that violence should be used offensively – a theoretical position rarely acted upon – while the PCP viewed violence as a defensive measure, the deployment of which should be carefully calibrated to avoid counterproductive reprisals.

The MRPP adopted quasi-paradoxical positions on various occasions in order to pursue its criticism of the PCP. One FEML pamphlet, for instance, enthusiastically reported that some of its militants who were jailed in Peniche had won an important battle to improve prison conditions. Thus, as a result of a struggle initiated in 1970 they had conquered their first demand in 1972: 'the separation of revisionists and revolutionaries, with the latter moving to the second floor of B Pavilion'. However, the same pamphlet lamented that 'the patriots from the colonies are still forced to mix with the revisionist scum'.[21] What is more, in October 1972, when the student Ribeiro Santos died, the FEML affirmed that 'comrade Ribeiro Santos died serving the people in the struggle against fascism and revisionism, the ideology of the bourgeoisie disguised as working class ideology'.[22]

Hence, be it in theoretical or propaganda terms, combating revisionism was at least as important as the struggle against the regime. In the MRPP's reconstruction of its own history published on the third anniversary of its creation in September 1973, it was claimed that, 'for the first time in our country, the proletariat is organizing itself in a revolutionary way, independently of all organizations and agents of the bourgeoisie, which have been sabotaging the development of the consciousness of the Portuguese people for more than a century'.[23] According to the MRPP, the working class had been organized and led by reformists and liberals until 1921, and then by the PCP, which was 'communist in inverted commas, because in reality it was a party of the bourgeoisie that always had the goal of silencing the working class and tightening the chains around the body of the people'.[24] From 1953 onwards, 'after the death of the great Stalin', the PCP had started to fight the revisionism 'that had taken control of the direction of the Soviet CP through Khrushchev, with the aim of destroying socialism and reinstating capitalism'.[25]

The 'glorious Communist Party of China, with its great leader comrade Mao Zedong' was seen to head this struggle. It was stated that, from 1961 onwards, revisionism in Portugal had 'put on new garb to carry on with its mission to deceive the people, from which there emerged some four groups that called themselves anti-revisionist and communist but which were ultimately of the same kind'.[26] It was only in 1970 that the true disciples of Marx, Engels, Lenin, Stalin and Mao had organized with the creation of the MRPP, inaugurating a period of 'open clashes between the people and the bourgeoisie, a period of revolutionary action by the proletariat and the people, in the phase of direct preparation of the popular forces to overthrow the colonialist and fascist bourgeoisie'.[27]

In October 1973, the Caetano government held the second legislative elections, with the first having taken place after the disillusionment of the Marcelist Spring of 1969. That year, the EDE, from which various members of the MRPP had originated, had undertaken an intense electoral campaign in favour of the CDE; but in 1973 the results of the radicalization process became apparent, with the adoption of a strong anti-electoral stance, expressed in slogans such as 'the people vote on the streets' and 'out with the electoral farce'.

This anti-systemic position was maintained even after the authoritarian regime had fallen. The document of the MRPP, disclosed on the morning of 25 April 1974, highlights the level of radicalization of this student-based group. In it, the coup of the 'colonial-fascist army' was dismissed as 'a battle between two cliques of the dominant class', so that 'independently of the results of this reactionary struggle, neither the people nor the working class should raise their hopes in this fight and its result'. The only way to liberate the people and workers was through a 'popular democratic revolution: an armed popular revolution, initiated and carried forward by the people, under the strict supervision of the working class and its revolutionary party, a Marxist–Leninist party'.[28]

The Ancient Regime and the Revolution

Portugal in Transition

On 25 April 1974 the New State was overthrown by a peaceful military coup led by officers of the Permanent Staff. As mentioned earlier, they had previously set up the Captains' Movement, initially for professional reasons; thereafter, they established the MFA, which was clearly politicized and espoused the belief that the Colonial War would only end with the demise of the regime. On the night of 24/25 April, various military units took up strategic positions in Lisbon and, hours later, in Porto and other cities. The regime fell after a day of mobilization, negotiations and some incidents (such as some hours of resistance by PIDE/DGS agents in their headquarters, which resulted in four people being shot dead). Marcelo Caetano handed over power to General António Spínola at the Carmo headquarters of the GNR. On 26 April came the announcement of the creation of the Junta de Salvação Nacional (National Salvation Council, JSN), presided by Spínola. A decree-law was promulgated that dismissed the former government, dissolved the National Assembly, the PIDE/DGS, the Legião Portuguesa and the Mocidade Portuguesa, the organs of censorship and the single party, the ANP, and dismissed President Américo Tomás. At the same time, an amnesty was passed covering all political crimes, and the approximately 130 political prisoners who were held in Peniche and Caxias were released.

The impact of the coup transcended national borders in a world divided by the Cold War and deeply shaken by the recent oil crisis. Those who rushed to establish a parallel between events in Portugal and Chile a year earlier were quickly proved wrong (Rezola 2010). Against all predictions and models of military interventions in processes of transition and political change, the 'April Captains' presented a democratizing programme that included the establishment of a civilian government and free elections. After more than a decade of war on various fronts in Africa, the military unexpectedly initiated a process of decolonization that quickly culminated in the granting of independence to the former colonial peoples. This singular event caught the scholarly community by surprise, which then faced the difficult task of integrating the Portuguese case into the framework of analysis of transitional politics.

The MFA stated that its aim was not to take power but rather to guarantee that elections would be held within a reasonable time frame. For various reasons, however, this did not happen. Spínola had his own political project as laid out in his book, *Portugal e o Futuro* (Portugal and the Future), and evident in his stance during the discussion of the MFA Programme. His project became clear during his first public speeches: he wanted the establishment of a presidential regime, a gradual transition undertaken in a climate of social order and discipline, and a federative referendum-style solution to the colonial issue (Rezola 2010). These proposals clearly contradicted the MFA Programme, which called for Constituent Assembly elections within a year and, above all, the right of peoples to self-determination. Thus, the Captains abandoned their initial aim of handing over power after the toppling of the regime. The first clashes between the MFA and António de Spínola became fertile ground for the gradual transformation of the MFA into a political actor in the new political order (Rezola 2010).

The first provisional government (May–July 1974) still reflected the strong influence of Spínola and his project to rapidly extinguish the MFA.

But in the second provisional government, the military predominated over civilian elements and reflected the growing influence of the MFA. The JSN itself was strongly influenced by the MFA, particularly through Colonel Vasco Gonçalves, who was close to the PCP and was Prime Minister between the second and the fifth provisional governments (from 12 July 1974 to 19 September 1975). Gonçalves was responsible for the adoption of key social measures of the transitional period, including agrarian reform, the nationalization of key private enterprises (banks, insurance companies, public transports and iron works, among others), the introduction of a minimum wage for civil servants and, through Decree-Law 169-D/75 of 31 March, the institution of unemployment benefits. The tutelage of the MFA was also developed through other institutions: first the Programme Coordinating Commission established before the coup; then the Council of Twenty; followed by the MFA Assemblies; and finally the Council of the Revolution. The latter was only extinguished in 1982, which is why some scholars argued that the end of the transition and democratic consolidation only happened that year (Linz and Stepan 1996).

The MFA was not internally united or uniform: there were strong divergent currents from the outset, not least because of the influence of different parties and political groups. The current around Vasco Gonçalves who was close to the Communist Party had the greatest institutional influence, since Gonçalves was the Prime Minister during most of the provisional governments between July 1974 and September 1975. The Gonçalvist current played a leading role during the turbulent 'hot summer' of 1975, attempting to marginalize and institutionalize social conflicts and open clashes between the extreme left and right. However, Gonçalves was criticized both by moderate forces such as the PS and the PPD, which accused him of wanting to institute a socialist regime, and by radical forces, which accused him of not being revolutionary enough. The faction of the MFA was closer to the PS, while a third faction identified primarily with Otelo de Carvalho, who was connected with extreme left groups, particularly Maoist. Despite these conflicts within the MFA and between the movement and outside forces, the JSN managed to guide the country through the constituent assembly elections on 25 April 1975, as promised. Meanwhile, the Gonçalvista programme succumbed to extreme left and moderate opposition within the MFA. In September 1975, the fifth provisional government fell and the more moderate sixth provisional government was formed without Vasco Gonçalves and the Gonçalvistas.

On 25 November, a military coup attempt by officers close to the extreme left created a pretext for a countercoup by moderates, which put an end to the period of social agitation and to the Gonçalvista experiment.

Finally, on 25 April 1976, Portugal held its first ever democratic elections with universal suffrage, in which the PS gained the majority of the votes, followed by the centre-right, and in which the PCP affirmed itself as the country's fourth political force.

Power Falls to the Streets

The coup of 25 April 1974 was immediately followed by broad political and popular mobilization, in which all political and social forces expressed the various positions that had evolved during the last years of the regime. This turbulent period in contemporary Portuguese history, which was nominated as the PREC, was characterized by intense conflict between opposing political forces (mainly the extreme left, the extreme right and the conservatives), attempted coups and counter coups, massive social mobilization, the occupation of lands and factories, and the nationalization of private enterprises.

Thus, although Portuguese regime change triggered what was later called the third wave of democratization (Huntington 1991) the transition was characterized by elements of 'rupture' that were much more significant than those observed in the subsequent democratization processes in Spain and Greece (Linz and Stepan 1996; Costa Pinto 2006). As stressed before, the PREC has been considered as one of the periods of most intense mobilization in post-war Europe.[29]

Indeed, Linz and Stepan (1996) note how scholars often forget the degree of uncertainty that characterized regime change in Portugal, an observation also made by António Costa Pinto (2006), who underlines that various studies of the Portuguese transition are limited precisely because they take the outcome of the transition for granted. Moreover, contemporaneous reports and subsequent scholarly analyses also portray the ensuing popular mobilization as an exceptional phenomenon. In the words of Manuel Braga da Cruz, it was a mobilization with neither past nor future in the history of Portuguese politics. In his view, the high level of political and social engagement of the Portuguese population during the revolution was a consequence of political and social decompression, which had the effect of liberating accumulated tensions; but he adds that the ensuing demobilization shows that the underlying political culture had not changed.[30] Howard Wiarda shares this view: for him, historically, Portuguese political culture is non-participatory, except during the democratic transition, when the 'other Portugal' exploded into revolution (Wiarda 2006: 123).

In fact, some of the most important studies of Portuguese regime change have stressed the discontinuities between political participation and social mobilization during the transitional period, and the prior level of political engagement of the Portuguese population.[31] Thus, an essential challenge for social scientists dealing with the Portuguese revolutionary process has been to explain such broad levels of mobilization during the PREC. Philippe Schmitter suggests that we should see this phenomenon as an 'awakening' of civil society resulting from the institutional vacuum left after the coup d'état (Schmitter 1999).

As seen above, Durán Muñoz (2000) was the first scholar to use the concept of Political Opportunity Structure to explain the diffusion of mobilization. This concept has been fruitfully used by Palacios Cerezales (2003) in conjunction with Michel Dobry's (1986) theory of political crisis to analyse the Portuguese transition. Palacios Cerezales suggests that mobilization was stimulated by the loss of inter-institutional legitimization and the pulverization of coercive State power. Costa Pinto (2006) also has this interpretation, in referring to the 'window of opportunity' that permitted the mobilization of the revolutionary process.

All these analyses make a fundamental contribution to the study of the Portuguese case, and have the merit of integrating social movement theory into the theoretical framework and methodology deployed by the literature on transitions and democratization. However, it is also important to look at the pre-existing social conditions that may have opened up political opportunities; and at the mutual influence between institutional politics and social movements, and not just at the unilateral effects of the former on the latter. Thus, I concur with Manuel Villaverde Cabral when he states that the coup d'état that overthrew the dictatorship was not the 'last instance of social change' but rather 'it is social change that must explain the new attitudes of the military, albeit in mediated ways' (Villaverde Cabral 1983: 130). On this view, 'in historical perspective, the coup of the 25 April 1974, was an accelerator of a longer process of liberalization and modernization in the country despite, and against the inflexibility of, the authoritarian political system' (ibid.: 128).

This fits with a reinterpreted political opportunities' model, which suggests to look 'not only at the way in which the state players define the milieu in which individuals act but also the way protest groups help to modify the conditions in which individuals act' (Fillieule 2005: 213). Thus, while it is true that the opening of POS decisively favoured broad social mobilization during the PREC, it is also true that this mobilization had a 'recent past'. It was actually the peak of a cycle of protest that had begun in the 1960s and intensified in the 1970s. That cycle only ended in 1975 with the institutionalization of democracy, particularly after the 25 April 1975 elections for the Constituent Assembly and the end of the decolonization process. Popular participation during the PREC did not emerge in a vacuum; it was strictly related to the intense conflict during the final years of the regime, and was a motor for opening POS and bringing about the crisis of the State. As seen before, the end of the New State was in fact characterized by a pluralization of the social sectors involved in the conflict, which was expressed in a renewed repertoire of more radical action, including sabotage, damage to university installations, real attacks on the symbols of the regime (particularly military ones), and even apparently more peaceful actions, such as prayer vigils. However, even the most moderate actions, such as the vigil for peace (and hence against the Colonial War) held at Rato Chapel at the end of 1972, had an inflammatory effect. The gravest threat to the regime was agitation over the war, which made many social sectors uneasy.

Many of the movements that emerged during the final phases of the regime merged with those born immediately after the revolution. The clear case of continuity is the student movement. As described above, in 1973 it had protested in the poorest areas of Lisbon where shanty towns had emerged. In Boavista, student action prefigured the first house occupations in that neighbourhood undertaken on 2 May 1975 (Ramos Pinto 2007). Pedro Ramos Pinto shows that there was a direct connection between student mobilization at the end of the New State and the urban movements carrying out house occupations of the PREC period. He recalls a piece of oral history of the residents' commission in Quinta of the Fonsecas, related five years after the PREC:

> [A] few days after the coup, a group of local women decided to go and talk to some students from the nearby Law Faculty (a well-known centre of student opposition to the regime) to enlist their help in organizing a neighbourhood assembly. ... The women went to the Law Faculty perhaps inspired by the fact that the Police were always chasing the students, and the students always fighting back, with the lockouts at the universities – which were frequent occurrences before 25 April – and [confrontations with the Police] in front of the canteen or the Santa Maria Hospital. Many of the women worked in the hospital, others in the canteen, which is to say they had contact with the students. Then, after 25 April, there you go! They stepped forward! (Ramos Pinto 2007: 91–92)

This story illustrates the direct transmission of the repertoire of contentious politics (in this case protest assemblies) from the student to the neighbourhood movement. The assemblies were essential for the organization of housing occupations; they were also a novelty for people used to living under an authoritarian regime. Thus, the prior experience of students with contentious action was important for the development of the neighbourhood movements. This is not really surprising. As this chapter shows, growing conflict involving practically all social sectors marked 1973 and the first months 1974. Students played a dominant role in this, not least because of their radicalism. Indeed, students were among the most dangerous political actors for the regime in its final phase. They represented half of all political prisoners in 1973, the year with most student imprisonments in absolute numbers since 1956, and this dynamic continued during the first months of 1974.

Therefore, the universities can be seen as incubators of political radicalization in terms of ideology, protest content and methods of contestation (Accornero 2010, 2013a, 2013b). This process, which had begun in the 1960s, intensified at the beginning of the 1970s. As the archival material shows – the official press, police documents and, above all, the student press – it accelerated significantly from the end of 1972 onwards. The watershed moment in the process of escalation of conflict between students and authorities was the murder of José Ribeiro dos Santos by the PIDE/DGS on 12 October 1972. His funeral led to harsh clashes between students and the forces of law and order, and to imprisonments; and the memory of this death constituted a significant mobilization and radicalization factor in the years that followed. According to the radical student propaganda of the new left groups, the use of more extreme protest strategies was justified in response to the violence of the authorities.[32]

On the eve of 25 April 1974, student mobilization was therefore at the peak of its vitality and it was natural that it should continue during the revolutionary process. The continuities between mobilization at the end of the New State and during the first months after the revolution were also a product of the dissemination of a new repertoire of action and of new issues. Further, as was the case of MRPP militants, many of those fighting against the regime remained active after the latter's demise. This was primarily because students added an increasing number of social demands to their political ones. Students felt they were the ideal spokespeople of the underprivileged, whose living conditions they attributed not just to the dictatorial nature of the regime but also to the way in which capitalist society was organized. Thus, from 1967 and the Lisbon floods onwards, the student movement left the university and sought to establish links with 'the real country'.

During the revolution, students remained involved in struggles by other social sectors through new left groups, which radicalized political groups and modes of action. Demobilization only began in 1975 due to various institutional initiatives, the recomposition of State power, and the internal dynamics within student groups. The decline in mobilization was a result of the distancing of actors, growing competition between groups and the concomitant radicalization of protest, and the institutionalization of some actors and demands.

This became clear particularly after the elections to the Constituent Assembly on 25 April 1975, which inaugurated a gradual closure of opportunities for mobilization and opened the way for a return to government politics. Only a month after the elections, the dynamics of this closure were already becoming apparent, be it in terms of repressive strategies or the attempts to institutionalize and anchor the energies of activists through official channels. The first major repressive action, which served to reinstate the government's monopoly of political violence, occurred on 28 May 1975, when the Comando Operacional do Continente (Continental Operational Command, COPCON)[33] ordered the imprisonment of four hundred MRPP militants, among whom were many students and the MRPP leader, Arnaldo de Matos. The creation of the student civic service on 30 May 1975 aimed to channel student mobilization through institutional channels, allowing students to express their social concerns in a legitimate but also more controlled manner. One of the key aims of Decree-Law 270 75 was to 'ensure that students are more adequately integrated into Portuguese society and have broad contact with its problems, as well as a better understanding of the needs and lacks of the population',[34] but also to make sure that student activism would adapt itself to 'the needs of the population, the possibilities for cooperation of schools, and the framing capacity of public services and the current labour market'.[35] Thus, student participation, which had been self-managed until then, became a part of government planning.

The final phase of demobilization came on 25 November 1975 after the intense political radicalization of the 'hot summer', and the counter coup by moderate military officers in response to the alleged attempted coup by officers close to the radical left. This counter coup, which some see as the 'public sign of the triumph of officers who accepted the results of the elections of 25 April 1975 as the founding manifestation of the new democratic regime in Portugal' (Medeiros Ferreira 2001: 218) also marked the end of the PREC, the end of the crisis of the State, and the institutionalization of power away from 'the streets'. The 25 November, and the proclamation of Angolan independence two weeks later on 11 December, heralded the end of decolonization and of the protest cycle initiated in 1968, which had gained impetus during the last years of the regime with the politicization of the student movement – Portugal's future elite.

Notes

1. In 1960, the percentage of people employed in the primary sector was 43.6 per cent; in the secondary sector it was 28.7 per cent; and in the tertiary sector it was 27.7 per cent. The data for 1973 are 26, 36 and 37 per cent respectively. See Loff 2007: 150.

2. Data available at www.guerracolonial.org, and reproduced in Afonso and de Matos Gomes (2010: 479). According to these data, the peak of war expenditure was reached in 1968, when it accounted for 35 per cent of GDP.

3. The Brigadas Revolucionárias – and after the Partido Revolucionário do Proletariado (Revolutionary Party of the Proletariat, PRP) – was an extreme left-wing organization with Guevarrist leanings, established by student leaders during the academic crisis of 1962, which called for an armed struggle against the regime. In the last years of the New State it carried out acts of sabotage against military targets to favour the independence movements in the colonies.

4. The CEM was the Comissão Eleitoral Monárquica (Royalist Electoral Commission).

5. The Partido Popular Democrático (Popular Democratic Party, PPD), a Christian democratic party created on 6 May 1974, was legalized on 25 January 1975, and in 1976 changed its name to Partido Social Democrata (Social Democratic Party, PSD). To the right of the PSD was the nationalist, conservative and liberal Centro Democrático Social – Partido Popular (Social Democratic Centre – Popular Party, CDS-PP), founded on 19 July 1974.

6. See Decree-Law 353 73, article 1, at the AHM, division 1, section 39, box 1, document 59.

7. Dispatch of the Minister of Defence and the Army, Sá Viana Rebelo, on Decree-Law 353 73, in ibid., document 62.

8. Memorandum from the Director of Personnel of the Instituto de Altos Estudos Militares (Higher Institute of Military Studies, IAEM), 17 July 1973, in ibid., document 70.

9. *Diário de Notícias*, 17 May 1972.

10. This is where the Plenary Court, where political crimes were tried, was situated.

11. PIDE/DGS report on the funeral of Ribeiro dos Santos, 14 October 1972, in IAN/TT-PIDE/DGS-SC-SR-3529/62-3371-Pt.170, p. 234.

12. CEDL pamphlet.

13. PSP report on the events in the Boavista neighbourhood, 12 May 1973, in PIDE/DGS-SC-SR-3529/62-3371-Pt.170, p. 54.

14. Political prisoners are defined here as all citizens imprisoned by the PIDE/DGS or those delivered to the PIDE/DGS who were arrested by other police forces (the PSP, the PJ or the GNR). The database is based on PIDE/DGS files, which have information on around 85 per cent of all political prisoners between 1934 and 1974. It should be noted that the data are based on arrests not prisoners, so a new record is made each time the same person is arrested.

15. See IAN/TT, Political Prisoners File of the PIDE/DGS.

16. See IAN/TT-PIDE/DGS, SCC1(1) 5040 1287, document 53. These sentences were not fully enforced as the regime came to an end.

17. For a detailed picture of Portuguese Maoism, see Cardina 2010 and 2011.

18. PRP Communiqué read by Radio Portugal Livre on 23 October 1973, between 1:15 and 1:30 am; transcribed interception by the Tapping Services of the Portuguese Legion. IAN/TT-PIDE/DGS-SC-C1(2)-18327-7814, p. 21.
19. Coimbra PIDE/DGS report, 4 February 1974, in IAN/TT-PIDE/DGS-SC-SR-19313-7835, p. 1.
20. Ibid.
21. FEML pamphlet, 21 September 1972.
22. FEML pamphlet, October 1973.
23. MRPP leaflet, written on its third anniversary, September 1973.
24. Ibid.
25. Ibid.
26. Ibid.
27. Ibid.
28. Lenin Committee, 'Communiqué to the Portuguese People by the MRPP', issued at dawn on 25 April 1974.
29. See note 11.
30. For a critical analysis, see Palacios Cerezales (2003: 106–7).
31. See, among the others, Schmitter (1999), Palacios Cerezales (2003) and Durán Muñoz (2000).
32. As we know today, most of these declarations were just that. In the case of the MRPP in particular, revolutionary violence was limited to the destruction of some building fronts; and even in the case of the PRP one cannot speak of armed struggle at the level found in other democratic (e.g. Italy and Germany) and non-democratic (e.g. Spain) European countries. The conditions for armed struggle were there, but the reasons why armed violence was not systematically deployed is an open question that lies beyond the scope of this work.
33. The COPCON was a military command structure for Continental Portugal, which was part of the General Staff of the Armed Forces, established by the MFA in July 1974 to protect the transition and to implement the MFA Programme. For a time it was the only stable public law and order institution that was completely loyal to the government. Headed by Commander Otelo de Carvalho with five thousand soldiers, on 11 March 1975 it defeated an attempted coup by right-wing officers close to Spínola.
34. Decree-Law 270 75, article 1.
35. Decree-Law 270 75.

Conclusions

Social Movements and Authoritarianism

A Paradoxical Relationship

Throughout this work, I have above all examined the ways that the Portuguese student movement progressively constructed spaces of participation which, to some extent, influenced the actual political process. I have tried to show that the influence of social movements – and in this specific case of the student movement – was determinant at various stages of the final years of the New State, creating a series of fundamental conditions for this period of exceptional political and social participation recalled as the PREC.

As seen before, some studies which are milestones for the analysis of the PREC from the point of view of social mobilizations considered this period as an exceptional example of the opening of the political opportunity structure (Durán Muñoz 1997, 2000; Palacios Cerezales 2003; Costa Pinto 2006). On the other hand, Manuel Villaverde Cabral has interpreted this opening and the major post-revolutionary mobilization as the result of political processes dating from a more distant past, linked to the prolonged crisis of the Portuguese state, whose elites, especially military, were already divided on the solution to be given to the colonial issue (Villaverde Cabral 2008: 115). However, the military personnel who physically toppled the regime, creating the conditions for the opening of opportunities, were in turn also influenced by the processes of change fostered by the social mobilization of the final years of the regime (Villaverde Cabral 1983: 130). This finding is coherent with the dynamic interpretation of the concept of the political opportunity discussed previously.

As stated in the introduction, and underlined throughout this entire work, the student sector was one of the most radically mobilized and most politicized at the end of the regime, as well as one of the most dangerous to the regime's survival. It is important to emphasize that the danger of this movement was not as much derived from the student activism in itself, but from the waves it extended throughout many other sectors of society through a process of diffusion, interpreted, according to the definition given by Charles Tilly and Sidney Tarrow, as a mechanism of 'spread of a contentious performance, issue, or interpretive frame from one site to another' (Tilly and Tarrow 2006: 215). This mechanism is one of the most significant in protest cycles. Hence, it was not only the mobilization that spread, but also the whole series of issues, under the form of new social values, new behaviour and new relations that were extended. We have also analysed how this process inevitably and especially reached the armed forces, whose social and age composition was closest to that of the students. Furthermore, the different controversies linked to the Colonial War, such as the draft resistance movement, the long compulsory military service, the conscription of the most active students and, finally, the constant lack of men for the army, were particularly nerve-racking for the armed forces.

According to this interpretation, the major and unexpected popular participation in the revolutionary process was, therefore, not only the result of the contingent opening of political opportunities ushered in by the 25 April, but also the most visible effect of the resources, networks and repertoire tenaciously constructed during the protest cycle of opposition to the New State in the continuously careful use of the mobilizing possibilities conveyed by the political process. In fact, as Doug McAdam states:

> Changes in a system of institutionalized politics merely afford a potential challenger the opportunity for collective action. It is the organizational vehicles available to the group at the time the opportunity presents itself that condition its ability to exploit the new opening. In the absence of such vehicles, the group is apt to lack the capacity to act when afforded the opportunity to do so. (McAdam 1999: ix)

This wealth of resources, which were almost exclusively of the PCP up to the early 1960s, then began to be increasingly developed, and in a more radical manner, by the groups of the extreme left throughout the 1960s, 1970s and during the PREC.

Hence, the study of the Portuguese student movement, apart from being important in itself due to its specific historical characteristics, in my opinion allows us to reflect on issues linked to the possibilities of action, to restrictions and to the effects of social movements in a right-wing authoritarian context. Apart from being interesting from a macro perspective of mobilizations and social movements, the Portuguese case also appears to be very significant in an attempt to understand, at a more micro and meso level, the effects of militancy in a right-wing authoritarian context, both in terms of networks and individual militant trajectories. This is even more so if we consider the moment when the regime ended, a moment after which, once the revolutionary period had passed, not only the major social mobilizations that had characterized the cycle of protest dispersed, but many of the 'historic' militants of the opposition against the New State abandoned active militancy. The possibility of 'reinvesting' the skills acquired during militancy and resuming past projects of life, professional and family-based, that had been interrupted due to the repression, are some of the reasons underlying this process of 'disengagement'. In this sense, one could talk of a real 'authoritarian paradox' – in other words, while the regime intended to demobilize its opposition through repression, in many cases the effect, as explained above, was to make this demobilization impossible, until the moment of the actual democratic opening.

A micro-level analysis of militant life trajectories highlights this point more clearly. Let us look at the life of José Luís Saldanha Sanches, one of the most important student leaders who spent most of his militant career in detention under the New State. Sanches was a member of the PCP, who 'converted' to Maoism in 1966–1967 during his second and most prolonged period of detention at the Peniche political prison, where he came into contact with Maoist prisoners. Released in 1971, he returned to the Law Faculty and joined the MRPP and, due to this 'second militancy', he was again arrested twice before the fall of the regime, and at the time of the coup d'état he was being held at Caxias prison. Like other political prisoners, he was freed immediately after the coup, and became the first 'public face' of the MRPP. When the revolution began he was committed to the anti-systemic position of this organization, and for this he was arrested once again under the new regime. In fact, the new political dispensation did not immediately change his position or political action. Nevertheless, over the medium term, it allowed him to develop others social activities, both professional and family-related, and he began to distance himself from the MRPP and abandon political participation. This disengagement accompanied his return to the study of law, which he had been forced to suspend due to persecution by the regime, and then to start a new career as a journalist and university lecturer. The stories of political exiles returning to Portugal after the revolution are similar. The end of the regime enabled them to return home and undertake new professional, social or personal projects. At the same time, some ceased to be involved directly in political activities. Myriad micro-level trajectories such as these make up the process of macro-level demobilization, which scholars have observed as being a feature of life after the 'hot summer' (Accornero 2013a, 2013b, 2013c).

Use of the 'sociology of social movements' to analyse authoritarian or transitional situations – traditionally scantily explored by the scholars of this area (della Porta 2016) – can thus enable, in my perspective, the discovery and illumination of facets of process of mobilization and militant trajectories than have hitherto not emerged due to exclusive concentration of democratic contexts. It is difficult to say whether the knowledge achieved on mobilization processes through a study of this type can be generalizable, but they can very probably at least enable comparisons with both similar and different situations. While on the one hand the use of tools of the sociology of social movements in authoritarian contexts can help us to better understand some aspects of the processes of mobilization, on the other side I would like to believe that the actual specific case of the Portuguese student movement during the final years of the New State – apart from being important in its own right due to its particularities – can help in some manner to renovate various aspects of this approach.

From an opposite point of view, we could say that 25 April was a real 'revolution in social science'. The political and social processes that preceded the fall of the regime, as well as the PREC, represented a kind of 'laboratory' for scholars of various areas – above all for scholars of social movements, as we have seen. The Portuguese revolution represented a social and political rupture, a founding moment, and opened the possibility for the development of various fields of studies in Portugal in the areas of sociology, political science and history, which had been censured and held back during the dictatorship. It also opened the door for studies on the role of social conflict and class struggle in the country's history – which had of course been completely absent during the dictatorship – and ended up by becoming a new field of research in which social movements theory was applied for the first time.

There are many potentialities in Portugal for the development of social science in the specific area of the study of conflict and social movements. Apart from the issues that emerged from a long dictatorship and a revolutionary transition process, highlighted throughout this study, I would like to make a final point. While Portugal is frequently considered as a peripheral European country, its geographic, historical and linguistic position could rightly make it a common ground for crossing different traditions of thought, such as those of Brazil, Portuguese-speaking Africa and Asia, and Europe. In this sense, it seems significant that alternative approaches to the study of social movements are strongly rooted, as is the case of James Scott's work or the 'Epistemology of the South' developed by Boaventura de Sousa Santos.

I believe Portuguese research on social movements would benefit greatly from communication among the different paradigms. Finally, I consider that Portugal's specific geographic, historical and linguistic circumstances mean that it has the potential to be a key centre for cross-fertilization among the different approaches and traditions. This reflection is even more pertinent if we consider the spread of the Portuguese language, which is spoken on four continents by about 240 million people and is the sixth most-spoken language in the world. This cross-fertilization process could give rise to new perspectives of social movements analysis, and attention could be drawn to contexts that are often almost overlooked by social movements scholars, such as African countries like Angola and Mozambique where there has been a strong wave of protests in recent years.

Finally, it is important to emphasize that the objective of this study, beyond drawing up the issues presented in these brief conclusions, was to search for new paths of research in relation to the study of social movements in Portugal. This objective will be achieved if other researchers are able to find in this work inspiration and questions for further research.

Lisbon, 18 January 2015

Bibliography

Accornero, G. 2010. 'La rivoluzione prima della rivoluzione', *Storia e Problemi Contemporanei* 54: 35–55.

Accornero, G. 2013a. 'La répression politique sous l'Estado Novo au Portugal et ses effets sur l'opposition estudiantine, des années 1960 à la fin du régime', *Cultures & Conflits* 89: 93–112.

Accornero, G. 2013b. 'A mobilização estudantil no processo de radicalização política durante o Marcelismo', *Análise Social* 48(208): 572–91.

Accornero, G. 2013c. 'Contentious Politics and Student Dissent in the Twilight of the Portuguese Dictatorship: Analysis of a Protest Cycle', *Democratization* 20(6): 1036–55.

Accornero, G. 2014. 'As medidas de repressão e criminalização política durante o Estado Novo Português e os seus efeitos nas trajectórias militantes', in I. Flunser Pimentel and I. Rezola (eds), *Democracia e Ditadura. Memória e Justiça Política*. Lisbon: Tinta da China, pp. 315–34.

Accornero, G., and G. Adinolfi. 2014. 'A Constituição do Estado Novo', in A. Belchior (ed.), *1911–2011 – Um Século de Constituições Republicanas: Direitos Fundamentais e Representação Política*. Lisbon: Mundos Sociais, pp. 65–83.

Accornero, G., and M. Villaverde Cabral. 2011. 'Saldanha Sanches militante', in F. Araújo and J.Taborda da Gama (eds), *Evocações do Prof. Doutor J.L. Saldanha Sanches*. Coimbra: Coimbra Editora, pp. 17–46.

Adinolfi, G. 2007. *Ai confini del fascismo. Propaganda e consenso nel Portogallo sala zarista*. Milan: Franco Angeli.

Afonso, A. and C. de Matos Gomes. 2010. *Os anos da guerra colonial, 1961–1975*. Matosinhos: QuidNovi.

Agosti, A., N. Tranfaglia and L. Passerini (eds). 1991. *La cultura e i luoghi del '68*. Milan: F. Angeli.

Almeida de Carvalho, R. 2004. 'O Marcelismo à luz da revisão constitucional de 1971', in F. Rosas and P. Aires Oliveira (eds), *A transição falhada: o marcelismo e o fim do Estado Novo (1968–1974)*. Lisbon: Notícias, pp. 27–89.

Almeida, J.M. 2008. *A oposição católica ao Estado Novo*. Lisbon: Edições Nelson de Matos.

Amado, C. 1998. 'A escola única em Portugal', in M. Cândida Proença (ed.), *O Sistema de Ensino em Portugal*. Lisbon: Colibri, pp. 87–111.

Barbosa, M. 2008. *Que força é essa*. Lisbon: Sextante.

Barreto, A. (ed.). 2000. *A Situação Social Em Portugal, 1960–1999*. Lisbon: ICS.

Barreto, J. 1990. 'Os primórdios da Intersindical sob Marcelo Caetano', *Análise Social* 25(105/106): 57–117.

Bebiano, R., and M. Manuela Cruzeiro. 2006. *Anos Inquietos: vozes do movimento estudantil em Coimbra (1961–1974)*. Porto: Afrontamento.

Benamor Duarte, M. 1997. 'Foi apenas um começo. A crise académica de 1969 na história do movimento estudantil dos anos Sessenta e da luta contra o Estado Novo', MA dissertation. Lisbon: Universidade Nova de Lisboa.

Bermeo, N. 1986. *The Revolution within the Revolution: Workers' Control in Rural Portugal*. Princeton, NJ: Princeton University Press.

Bermeo, N. 2007. 'War and Democratization: Lessons from the Portuguese Experience', *Democratization* 14(3): 388–406.

Braga da Cruz, M. 1995. *Instituições políticas e processos sociais*. Venda Nova: Bertrand.

Braga da Cruz, M. 2001. 'O CADC – Um Século de História', retrieved 5 May 2014 from http://www.cadc.pt/site/I_CENTENARIO.html.

Bruneau, T. 1989. 'Portugal's Unexpected Transition', in K. Maxwell and M. Haltzel (eds), *Portugal: Ancient Country, Young Democracy*. Washington, DC: Woodrow Wilson Center Press, pp. 9–23.

Caiado, N. 1990. *Movimentos estudantis em Portugal: 1945–1980*. Lisbon: Instituto de Estudos para o Desenvolvimento.

Canali, M. 2004. *Le spie del regime*. Bologna: Il Mulino.

Cardina, M. 2008. *A tradição da contestação. Resistência Estudantil em Coimbra no Marcelismo*. Coimbra: Angelus Novus.

Cardina, M. 2009. 'Olhares sobre uma ausência: o movimento estudantil no Estado Novo e o feminismo', in *Latitudes* 34, retrieved 2 April 2014 from http://www.ces.uc.pt/cesfct/mc/miguelcardina3.pdf#page=1&zoom=auto,0,491.

Cardina, M. 2010. *A esquerda radical*. Coimbra: Angelus Novus.

Cardina, M. 2011. *Margem de certa maneira. O maoísmo em Portugal, 1964–1974*. Lisbon: Tinta da China.

Carrilho, M. 1985. *Forças armadas e mudança política em Portugal no séc. XX: para uma explicação sociológica do papel dos militares*. Lisbon: Imprensa Nacional Casa da Moeda.

Cazzullo, A. 2006. *I ragazzi che volevano fare la rivoluzione*. Milan: Sperling & Kupfer.

Costa, J. 2002. 'O ano da morte de Ribeiro Santos', *História* 24(49): 21–28.

Costa Pinto, A. 2001. *O fim do império português. A cena internacional, a guerra colonial e a descolonização*. Lisbon: Livros Horizonte.

Costa Pinto, A. 2006. 'Authoritarian Legacies, Transitional Justice and State Crisis in Portugal's Democratization', *Democratization* 13(2): 173–204.

Cunhal, Á. 1970. *O radicalismo pequeno-burguês de fachada socialista*. Lisbon: Edições Avante!

Davenport, C., C. Mueller and H. Johnston. 2005. *Repression and Mobilization*. Minneapolis: University of Minnesota Press.

Della Porta, D. (2016). 'Mobilizing for Democracy: The 1989 Protests in Central Eastern Europe', in G. Accornero and O. Fillieule, *Social Movements Studies in Europe: The State of the Art*. New York and Oxford: Berghahn Books, pp. 57-81.

Della Porta, D., and H. Reiter. 2003. *Polizia e protesta. L'ordine pubblico dalla Liberazione ai «no global»*. Bologna: Il Mulino.

Dobry, Michel. 1986. *Sociologie des crises politiques*. Paris: Presses de la FNSP.

Durán Muñoz, R. 1997a. 'As crises económicas e as transições para a democracia. Espanha e Portugal numa perspectiva comparada', *Análise Social* 32(141): 369–401.

Durán Muñoz, R. 1997b. 'Oportunidad para la transgresión. Portugal, 1974–1975', *Ler História* 32: 83–116.

Durán Muñoz, R. 2000. *Contención y transgresión. Las movilizaciones sociales y el Estado en las transiciones española y portuguesa*. Madrid: Centro de Estudios Políticos y Constitucionales.

Durkheim, E. 1995. *The Elementary Forms of Religious Life*. New York: The Free Press.

Eisinger, P. 1973. 'The Conditions of Protest Behavior in American Cities', *American Political Science Review* 67: 11–28.

Estado-Maior de Exército. Comissão para o Estudo das Campanhas de Africa. 1988. *Resenha histórico-militar das Campanhas de África (1961–1974)*. Lisbon: EME.

Fernandes, T. 2006. *Nem ditadura, nem revolução. A ala liberal e o Marcelismo (1968–1974)*. Lisbon: Dom Quixote.

Fillieule, O. 1997. *Stratégies de la rue: les manifestations en France*. Paris: Presses de Science Po.

Fillieule, O. 2005. 'Requiem pour un concept Vie et mort de la notion de structure des opportunités politiques', in G. Dorronsoro, *La Turquie Conteste. Mobilisation Sociales et Regimes Securitaire*. Paris: CNRS Éditions, pp. 201–18.

Fillieule, O. 2010. 'Some Elements of an Interactionist Approach to Political Disengagement', *Social Movements Studies* 9(1): 1–15.

Flunser Pimentel, I. 2007a. *A História da Pide*. Lisbon: Círculo de Leitores.

Flunser Pimentel, I. 2007b. *Mocidade Portuguesa Feminina*. Lisbon: A Esfera dos Livros.

Garrido, Á. 1996. *Movimentos estudantis e crise do Estado Novo: Coimbra 1962*. Coimbra: Minerva.

Grandi, A. 2003. *La generazione degli anni perduti. Storie di Potere Operaio*. Turin: Einaudi.

Granja, P.J. 2002. 'Dos filmes sonoros ao cine-clubismo', *História* 47: 29–33.

Grupo de Trabalho Português do Projecto Regional do Mediterrâneo. 1963. *Análise quantitativa da estrutura escolar portuguesa (1950–1959).* Lisbon: Instituto de Alta Cultura.

Hammond, J.L. 1988. *Building Popular Power: Workers' and Neighborhood Movements in the Portuguese Revolution.* New York: Monthly Review Press.

Henry, C. 2006. *A cidade das flores. Para uma recepção cultural em Portugal do cinema neo-realista italiano como metáfora de uma ausência.* Lisbon: FCG and FCT.

Huntington, S. 1991. *Democracy's Third Wave.* Oklahoma: University of Oklahoma Press.

Iacuaniello, M., E. Pantano and E. Bollino. 2009. *Solidarietà e utopia. Bologna, gli angeli del fango e le alluvioni del 1966.* Bologna: Clueb.

Ivani, M. 2009. *Esportare il fascismo. Collaborazione di polizia and diplomazia culturale tra Italia fascista and Portogallo di Salazar (1928–1945).* Bologna: Clueb.

Klimke, M., and J. Scharloth (eds). 2008. *1968 in Europe: A History of Protest and Activism, 1956–77.* New York and London: Palgrave Macmillan.

Klimke, M., J. Pekelder and J. Scharloth (eds). 2011. *Between Prague Spring and French May: Opposition and Revolt in Europe, 1960–1980.* New York and Oxford: Berghahn Books.

Kornetis, K. 2013. *Children of Dictatorship: Student Resistance, Cultural Politics and the 'Long 1960s' in Greece.* New York and Oxford: Berghahn Books.

Kouki, H., and E. Romanos (eds). 2011. *Protest Beyond Borders: Contentious Politics in Europe since 1945.* New York and Oxford: Berghahn Books.

Linz, J., and A. Stepan. 1996. *Problems of Democratic Transition and Consolidation: Southern Europe, South America and Post-Communist Europe.* Baltimore, MD: Johns Hopkins University Press.

Loff, M. 2007. 'Marcelismo e ruptura democrática no contexto da transformação social portuguesa dos anos 1960–1970', *Espacio, Tiempo y Forma-Historia Contemporánea* 19(5): 145–84.

Lourenço, G., J. Costa and P. Pena. 2001. *Grandes Planos. Oposição estudantil à Ditadura: 1956–1974.* Lisbon: Âncora Editora.

Lucena, M. de. 1995. *O Regime Salazarista e a sua Evolução.* Matosinhos: Contemporânea Editora.

Madeira, J., I. Flunser Pimentel and L. Farinha. 2007. *Vítimas de Salazar. Estado Novo e violência política.* Lisbon: A Esfera dos Livros.

Maravall, J.M. 1978. *Dictatorship and Political Dissent: Workers and Students in Franco's Spain.* Basingstoke: Palgrave Macmillan.

Marwick, A. 1998. *The Sixties: Cultural Revolution in Britain, France, Italy, and the United States, 1958–1974.* New York: Oxford University Press.

Mazzone, U. 2006. 'Testimonianza di Umberto Mazzone', *Unibomagazine*, retrieved 6 May 2014 from http://www.magazine.unibo.it/Magazine/Bacheca/AngeliDelFango/2006/10/Testimonianza_Umberto_Mazzone.htm

McAdam, D. 1999. *Political Process and the Development of Black Insurgency, 1930–1970*. Chicago: Chicago University Press, 2nd edition.

McAdam, D., S. Tarrow and C. Tilly. 2001. *Dynamics of Contention*. Cambridge: Cambridge University Press.

Medeiros Ferreira, J. 1992. *O Comportamento político dos militares: Forças Armadas e regimes políticos em Portugal no século XX*. Lisbon: Estampa.

Medeiros Ferreira, J. 1998. 'O movimento estudantil nos anos Sessenta', in M. Cândida Proença, *Maio de 1968. Trinta anos depois. Movimentos Estudantis em Portugal*. Lisbon: Colibri, pp. 185–97.

Medeiros Ferreira, J. (ed.). 2001. *Portugal em transe*, Vol. 8 of J. Mattoso (ed.), *História de Portugal*. Lisbon: Estampa.

Morlino, L. 2003. *Democrazie e democratizzazioni*. Bologna: Il Mulino.

Narciso, R. 2000. *Acção Revolucionária Armada. A história secreta do braço armado do PCP*. Lisbon: Dom Quixote.

Nery, I. 2008. 'Cresce a repressão', *Visão História* 2: 32–34.

Ortoleva, P. 1988. *Saggio sui movimenti del 1968 in Europa e in America*. Rome: Editori Riuniti.

Pacheco Pereira, J. 2005. *Álvaro Cunhal. Uma biografia política*. Lisbon: Temas e Debates.

Pacheco Pereira, J. 2008. *O um dividiu-se em dois. Origens e enquadramento internacional dos movimentos pró-chineses e albaneses nos países ocidentais e em Portugal (1960–1965)*. Lisbon: Alêtheia.

Palacios Cerezales, D. 2003. *O Poder Caiu na rua. Crise de Estado e Acções Colectivas na Revolução Portuguesa, 1974–1975*. Lisbon: ICS.

Palacios Cerezales, D. 2011. *Portugal à coronhada. Protesto popular e ordem pública nos séculos XIX e XX*. Lisbon: Tinta da China.

Patriarca, M.F. 1995. *A questão social no salazarismo, 1930–1947*. Lisbon: Imprensa Nacional Casa da Moeda.

Patriarca, M.F. 2004. 'Estado Social. A caixa de Pandora', in F. Rosas and P. Aires Oliveira (eds), *A transição falhada: o marcelismo e o fim do Estado Novo (1968–1974)*. Lisbon: Notícias, pp. 171–212.

Patriarca, M.F. 2008. 'Continuidade e ruptura: as primeiras leis de Marcello Caetano', in M. Villaverde Cabral et al. (eds). *Itinerários – A investigação nos 25 anos do ICS*. Lisbon: ICS, pp. 125–39.

Pereira, V. 2012. *La dictature de Salazar face à l'émigration. L'Etat portugais et ses migrants en France (1957–1974)*. Paris: Presses de Sciences Po.

Proença, M.C. 2004. 'A reforma educativa de Veiga Simão', in F. Rosas and P. Aires Oliveira (eds), *A transição falhada: o marcelismo e o fim do Estado Novo (1968–1974)*. Lisbon: Notícias, pp. 233–58.

Ramos Pinto, P. 2007. 'Urban Protest and Grassroots Organisations in Lisbon, 1974–1976', Ph.D. dissertation. Cambridge: University of Cambridge.

Ramos Pinto, P. 2013. *Lisbon Rising: Urban Social Movements in the Portuguese Revolution, 1974–75*. Manchester: Manchester University Press.

Rezola, M.I. 2010. 'Il Movimento delle Forze Armate e la transizione verso la democrazia', *Storia e Problemi Contemporanei* 54: 35–55.

Rodrigues, L.N. 1996. *A Legião Portuguesa: a milícia do Estado Novo (1936–1944)*. Lisbon: Editorial Estampa.

Rosas, F. (ed.). 1997. *O Estado Novo*. Vol. 7 of J. Mattoso (ed.), *História de Portugal*. Lisbon: Estampa.

Rosas, F. 2004. *Portugal Século XX. Pensamento e Acção Política*. Lisbon: Notícias.

Rosas, F. 2008. 'Prefácio', in J. Miguel Almeida, *A oposição católica ao Estado Novo*. Lisbon: Edições Nelson de Matos, pp. iii-ix.

Rosas, F. (ed.). 2009. *Tribunais Políticos. Tribunais Militares Especiais e Tribunais*. Lisbon: Temas e Debates.

Rosas, F. 2012. '1962, ano de fronteira', in *100 dias que abalaram o regime. A crise académica de 1962*. Lisbon: Tinta da China, pp. 27–35.

Rosas, F., and P. Aires Oliveira (eds). 2004. *A transição falhada: o marcelismo e o fim do Estado Novo (1968–1974)*. Lisbon: Notícias.

Sabino, A.L., et al. 2009. *À Espera de Godinho*. Lisbon: Bizâncio.

Schmitter, P. 1997. 'Clarifying Consolidation', *Journal of Democracy* (8)2: 168–74.

Schmitter, P. 1999. *Portugal do Autoritarismo à Democracia*. Lisboa: ICS.

Schmitter, P. 2014. 'Reflections on "Transitology" – Before and After', in D. Brinks, M. Leiras and S. Mainwaring (eds), *Reflections on Uneven Democracies: The Legacy of Guillermo O'Donnell*. Baltimore, MD: Johns Hopkins University Press, pp. 71-86.

Seidelman, R. 1979. 'Neighborhood Communism in Florence: Goals and Dilemmas of the Italian Road to Socialism'. Ph.D. dissertation. Ithaca, NY: Cornell University.

Sousa Santos, B. de, 1990. *O Estado e a Sociedade em Portugal*. Porto: Afrontamento.

Strippoli, G. 2013. *Il partito e il movimento. Comunisti europei alla prova del Sessantotto*. Roma: Carrocci.

Tarrow, S. 1989. *Democracy and Disorder: Protest and Politics in Italy, 1965–1975*. Oxford: Oxford University Press.

Tarrow, S. 1998. *Power in Movement: Social Movements, Collective Action and Politics*. Cambridge: Cambridge University Press.

Teles Pereira, J.A. 1999. 'Medidas de Segurança', in A. Barreto and M.F. Mónica (eds), *Dicionário de História de Portugal vol. 8*. Lisbon: Livraria Figueirinha, p. 442.

Tiago de Oliveira, L. 2004. *Estudantes e Povo na Revolução. O serviço Cívico Estudantil (1974–1977)*. Lisbon: Celta.

Tilly, C. 1978. *From Mobilization to Revolution*. Chicago: Addison-Wesley.
Tilly, C. 1986. *The Contentious French*. Cambridge, MA: Harvard University Press.
Tilly, C. 1993. *European Revolutions, 1492–1992*. Oxford: Blackwell.
Tilly, C. 2006. *Regimes and Repertoires*. Chicago: Chicago University Press.
Tilly, C., and S. Tarrow. 2006. *Contentious Politics*. Boulder, CO: Paradigm Publishers.
Ungari, P. 1963. *Alfredo Rocco e l'ideologia giuridica del fascismo*. Brescia: Morcellina.
Ungari, P. 2002. *Storia del diritto di famiglia in Italia: 1796–1975*. Bologna: Il Mulino.
Vieira, J. 2008. *Mocidade Portuguesa*. Lisbon: A Esfera dos Livros.
Villaverde Cabral, M. 1983. 'A segunda república portuguesa numa perspectiva histórica', *Análise Social* 19(75): 127–42.
Villaverde Cabral, M. 2008. 'O 25 de Abril em retrospectiva', in A. Torres and L. Baptista (eds), *Sociedades Contemporâneas. Reflexividade e acção*. Porto: Afrontamento, pp. 113–21.
Wiarda, H.J. (ed.) 2006. *Development on the Periphery: Democratic Transitions in Southern and Eastern Europe*. Lanham, MD: Rowman & Littlefield.

SOURCES

Libraries

- National Library of Portugal (Lisbon)
- Central National Library (Rome)
- Library of the Centre of Advanced Studies in Social Science, Juan March Foundation (Madrid)

Archives

- Hemeroteca Municipal (Lisbon Municipal Newspaper, Journal and Magazine Library)
- Military History Archive (AHM, Lisbon)
- Social History Archive of the Social Science Institute of Lisbon University (AHS-ICS/UL), Student Movement Fund
- Torre do Tombo National Archive Institute (IAN/TT), Archive of the Ministry of Internal Administration (MI), 'Record of the Received Correspondence, 1956–1974', 19 volumes
- Torre do Tombo National Archive Institute (IAN/TT), PIDE/DGS Archive
- Torre do Tombo National Archive Institute (IAN/TT), PIDE/DGS Archive, Political Prisoners File

Index

www.ingramcontent.com/pod-product-compliance
Lightning Source LLC
Chambersburg PA
CBHW070931030426
42336CB00014BA/2630